EGYPT

ABDO
Publishing Company

EGYPT

by Val Karlsson

Content Consultant
Devin Stewart
Associate Professor of Arabic and Islamic Studies
Department of Middle Eastern and South Asian Studies, Emory University

CREDITS

Published by ABDO Publishing Company, 8000 West 78th Street, Edina, Minnesota 55439. Copyright © 2012 by Abdo Consulting Group, Inc. International copyrights reserved in all countries. No part of this book may be reproduced in any form without written permission from the publisher. The Essential Library™ is a trademark and logo of ABDO Publishing Company.

Printed in the United States of America,
North Mankato, Minnesota
062011
092011

 THIS BOOK CONTAINS AT LEAST 10% RECYCLED MATERIALS.

Editor: Erika Wittekind
Copy Editor: Susan M. Freese
Series design and cover production: Emily Love
Interior production: Kazuko Collins

About the Author: Val Karlsson is a freelance editor and writer based in Medford, Massachusetts. She has a bachelor of arts degree in comparative literature from the University of Massachusetts at Amherst. Most of her work involves developing print and internet-based academic materials for children, teens, and adults learning English or Spanish. She has also written a reference piece about Tunisia and a short horror novel.

Library of Congress Cataloging-in-Publication Data
Karlsson, Val.
  Egypt / by Val Karlsson.
    p. cm. -- (Countries of the world)
  Includes bibliographical references and index.
  ISBN 978-1-61783-108-9
  1. Egypt--Juvenile literature. I. Title.
  DT49.K37 2012
  962--dc22

               2011020090

Cover: The Pyramids of Giza

TABLE OF CONTENTS

CHAPTER 1
A VISIT TO EGYPT

You have just stepped out of a time machine—or so it seems. All around you are the traces of ancient wonders, medieval splendor, colonial rule, and modern industrial and commercial development. You have just arrived in Cairo, Egypt— one of the world's greatest ancient civilizations and one of the largest, most densely populated modern cities in Africa and the Middle East. You're familiar,

"I arrived at length at Cairo, mother of cities and seat of Pharaoh the tyrant, mistress of broad regions and fruitful lands, boundless in multitude of buildings, peerless in beauty and splendor, the meeting-place of comer and goer, the halting-place of feeble and mighty, whose throngs surge as the waves of the sea, and can scarce be contained in her for all her size and capacity."[1]

—Ibn Battuta, fourteenth-century Muslim traveler

The Great Sphinx, located near the Pyramids of Giza, was carved out of limestone.

of course, with ancient Egypt and some of its major symbols and personalities: the Pyramids, the Sphinx, mummies, Pharaoh Tutankhamen, Cleopatra, hieroglyphics. But what is modern Egypt like?

It's sunny, hot, and dry as you make your way down the bustling sidewalks of downtown Cairo. Dusty sand blown in from the desert settles everywhere, including on your shoes and even in your eyes. Street vendors hawk their wares, while child vendors weave through the streets selling gum or other small items. Occasionally, you may see a man rush past with a large basket of bread balanced on his head or perhaps even an old man driving a herd of goats!

The Egyptian people are warm and friendly and are generally happy to meet Americans. They may even try to talk to you or offer to show you around. Some will, of course, see an opportunity to sell you something or earn a tip, but you will find that many Egyptians are simply interested in talking to foreigners.

THE OLD AND THE NEW

Everywhere you go as you push through the crowds, you encounter old traditions mixed with new. You look up to notice the grand, classic European-style buildings designed by French and English settlers in the nineteenth and early twentieth centuries. Many of these buildings now house chic, modern storefronts and Western-style restaurants, while

The Khan al-Khalili bazaar in Cairo

THE CALL TO PRAYER

In Islamic countries such as Egypt, mosques broadcast the call to prayer, or *adhan*, five times a day. Muezzins can be heard singing out the *adhan* in sustained, booming tones from every mosque, starting at sunrise. In days past, the muezzins climbed to the top of minarets to give the call, using sheer vocal power to project their message. In modern times, they began using loudspeakers to reach their widespread, urban audience.

In Cairo, where there are approximately 4,000 mosques, the call to prayer could be quite loud. Many people found the sound beautiful and harmonious, while others found it chaotic and noisy. Still others complained of muezzins with bad voices. In 2010, a controversial plan was enacted to electronically rig all of the mosques to broadcast one single, unified call to prayer. Many Egyptians and visitors who appreciated the old tradition, as well as muezzins who worried about losing their jobs, opposed the change.

In recent years, it has become a fad for Muslims to use the call to prayer as their cell phone's ringtone. In January 2010, mufti Ali Gomaa issued a fatwa, or religious edict, condemning the practice and calling it "confusing and misleading," since someone could conceivably hear a phone ringing and mistake it for the real call to prayer.[2]

others have lost their original splendor due to the effects of time and neglect. Young men wearing jeans pass by, joking with each other, and young women wear stylish head scarves and modern yet modest Western-style clothing. You may also see older men in *gallibiyas*, or traditional Egyptian robes, and skullcaps smoking water pipes in coffee shops, playing backgammon, or engaging in deep discussion. The smell of apple-flavored tobacco wafting from their pipes is everywhere and unmistakable.

Cairo's streets are as teeming with vehicles as its sidewalks are with people. Cars, buses, and mopeds glut the streets, causing frequent traffic jams. The air

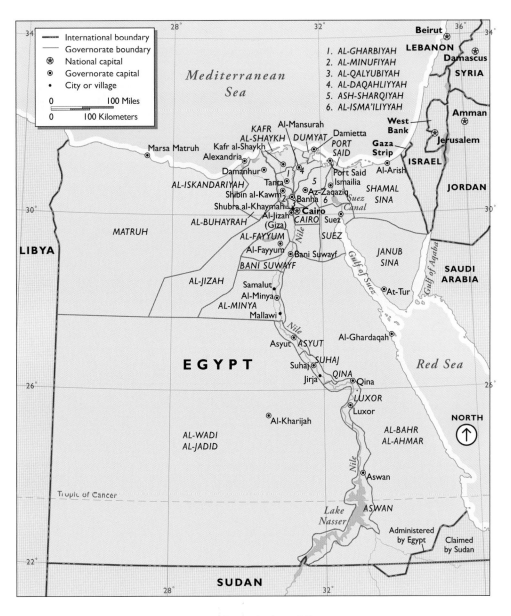

Political Boundaries of Egypt

is filled with the rumble of engines and the constant honking of horns. If you need to cross the street—look out! Crosswalks and crossing signals are rare, and most local people cross where and when they need to.

THE MUSEUM OF EGYPTIAN ANTIQUITIES

The Museum of Egyptian Antiquities in Cairo houses more than 120,000 treasures from the ancient Egyptian world, including statues, papyrus scrolls, sarcophagi, jewelry, masks, coins, and more. French architect Marcel-Lazare Dourgnon (1858–1911) designed the stately salmon-colored building in 1897 in the neoclassical style, and it opened in 1902. A special room features a dazzling collection of 11 royal mummies in refrigerated cases. The museum attracts millions of visitors each year.

Finally, you reach Islamic Cairo, or Old Cairo, the city's medieval center. Here, the skyline is sprinkled with minarets and domes of the mosques and palaces built during the periods of Arab and Turkish rule beginning in the seventh century. This is the site of the tenth-century al-Azhar University, which is touted by some as the world's oldest Islamic university. Get ready to be enchanted by the vibrant and charming Khan al-Khalili souk, or bazaar, where you can find jewelry, perfume, clothing, handicrafts, shoes, souvenirs, and more in the winding alleyways constructed in the fourteenth century. Delve deeper into the market, and you will find traditional and less touristy areas, such as the old spice market, where vendors dump mountains of powdered spices out of enormous bags, sending clouds of fragrant cumin and fenugreek into the air.

ANCIENT HERITAGE

Photos of the Pyramids of Giza always give the impression they are way out in the desert, surrounded by nothing but miles of sand, but actually, they are right next to Cairo. The ancient cities of Heliopolis and Memphis, on either side of the Nile River, are now suburbs of the modern city. The Pyramids of Giza and the even older step pyramid of Saqqarah were the burial tombs of the pharaohs of Memphis. Take just a short ride from the city by train, bus, car, or cab, and you can ride a camel around the towering ancient structures. The largest, the Great Pyramid built for King Khufu, is more than 4,500 years old.

If you are interested in seeing some of the treasures of ancient Egypt collected from Giza and other locations around the country, then your next destination should be the Museum of Egyptian Antiquities, next to Cairo's bus terminal. There, you can see incredible artifacts such as Tutankhamen's famous gold funerary mask and a collection of well-preserved ancient mummies—including the withered bodies of Ramses II and Queen Hatshepsut. And since the museum is next to the bus station, when you exit, you will be ready to embark on your next adventure—perhaps to the ancient seaport city of Alexandria in the north or to the ancient sites of Luxor and Aswan in the south.

Muslim protesters engage in prayer on February 11, 2011,
in Cairo's Tahrir Square.

ON THE HEELS OF A REVOLUTION

Your explorations of ancient Egypt may help you understand what is happening in the country today. A revolution in early 2011 resulted in ousting the authoritarian regime of President Hosni Mubarak and sending the country into a tense period of transition. Frustrated by the nation's limited economic opportunities and authoritarian rule, thousands of Egyptians took to the streets in protest. In January 2011, people worldwide watched in amazement as massive demonstrations took place—the largest Egypt had seen in years. The demonstrations were largely peaceful, but many Egyptians were arrested, wounded, or killed in clashes with police. The nation's military sided with the Egyptian people, which led President Mubarak to officially resign on February 11, following 18 suspenseful days.

The leaders of the newly installed military government promised to meet many of the protesters' demands. They committed to hold democratic elections within six months and to revise the country's constitution. While it was unclear whether military leaders would follow

"In Egypt, you see, our disease is the lack of democracy. . . . Poverty, injustice, even corruption, fanaticism, and even terrorism could be serious complications of the disease. There is no way to cure the symptoms and complications without curing the disease."[3]

—'Ala' al-Aswani, Egyptian author

Egyptians waving their national flag celebrate in Tahrir Square in downtown
Cairo on February 12, 2011, one day after President Hosni Mubarak resigned.

through on these plans—or who would ultimately end up in power—the
Egyptian people were hopeful that their country would finally achieve
democracy.

SNAPSHOT

Official name: Arab Republic of Egypt (in Arabic, Jumhuriyat Misr al-Arabiyah)

Capital city: Cairo

Form of government: Republic

Titles of leaders: Prime minister (head of government); president (chief of state)

Currency: Egyptian pound

Population (July 2011 est.): 82,079,636
World rank: 15

Size: 386,662 square miles (1,001,450 sq km)
World rank: 30

Language: Arabic

Official religion: Islam

Per capita GDP (2010, US dollars): $6,200
World rank: 136

CHAPTER 2

GEOGRAPHY: LAND OF THE NILE

Egypt's landscape consists largely of sprawling desert, dotted with oases and split by the Nile River and the narrow, fertile strips of land that line both its banks. The longest river in the world, stretching 4,000 miles (6,437 km) from eastern Africa to the Mediterranean Sea, the Nile is what made the great ancient civilization of Egypt possible. Its annual flooding left deposits of rich, fertile soil, carried north to Egypt from Ethiopia, and also washed away salts that would have made farming difficult.

Thus, the ancient Egyptians were able to flourish, developing an agricultural society that was surrounded by desert and therefore protected from easy attack by outsiders. The ancient Egyptians thought of their country as being divided into two regions: the red land (the sand of

The Nile River flows from south to north.

The Nile River at Aswan

THE ANNUAL NILE FLOOD

In ancient Egypt, the rhythm of life was regulated by the annual flooding of the Nile River. The river would begin rising in early summer, and it would flood by late summer or early fall, leaving behind wet, fertile soil ready for planting. This meant that the planting season occurred after the hottest months of the year. Because of this timetable, farming was easier for the Egyptians than for most other farmers of the time, whose rivers overflowed in the spring. The Egyptian harvest season was celebrated with parades, music, feasting, and religious rites honoring Min, the god of fertility.

The exact time of the flooding and the amount of the flooding varied, and the lack or overabundance of water could be devastating to the ancient Egyptians. However, they devised many systems of damming and irrigation to help control the waters of the Nile.

Since the 1960s, when the government built the Aswan High Dam, the Nile River has not flooded. However, the historic annual flood is still celebrated every August in the two-week Wafaa' al-Nil festival in Cairo, and the ancient harvest rites live on in Shamm al-Nasim, a celebration of spring honored by both Christian and Muslim Egyptians.

the desert) and the black land (the rich, fertile soil of the Nile valley).

Egypt is located in the northeast corner of the African continent but also claims a tiny wedge of Asia, the Sinai Peninsula. The nation is bordered by Libya to the west, Sudan to the south, and Israel and the Gaza Strip to the northeast. The Mediterranean Sea lies to the north, and the Red Sea lies to the east, with Saudi Arabia just on the other side.

Egypt is divided into 29 governorates, or administrative regions, with 217 cities and 4,617 villages.[1] Its principal cities by population are Cairo, the capital, followed by Alexandria in the north,

Giza and Shubra al-Khaymah, Hulwan, Port Said, Suez, Al-Mahallah al-Kubra, Al-Mansurah, Tanta, Asyut, Aswan, and Al-Fayyum.

GEOGRAPHIC FEATURES

Egypt occupies approximately 386,662 square miles (1,001,450 sq km), 97 percent of which is desert.[2] Approximately 6 percent of the nation's land is inhabited.[3] Only 3 percent is arable, meaning that it is fit for cultivation.[4] Egypt can be divided into five geographic regions: the Nile valley, the Nile delta, the Western Desert, the Eastern Desert, and the Sinai Peninsula.

ALEXANDRIA

The bustling coastal town of Alexandria was once the wonder of the Western world. In the third century BCE, Ptolemy established a great library/museum and center for scholarship in the city. It attracted the brightest minds of the age, such as Euclid, father of geometry, mathematician Archimedes, and Claudius Ptolemy, the father of astronomy and geography. The city also amassed the largest collection of books and scrolls the world had ever known—400,000 scrolls, by some accounts.[5] Tragically, by the seventh century CE, Alexandria had faded from glory, and the great library had burned. Most of its treasures of ancient knowledge were lost to the world.

The Nile valley is made up of the narrow strips of fertile land that lay on both sides of the Nile River, from the first cataract near Aswan in the south to Cairo. From Cairo, the river flows north toward the

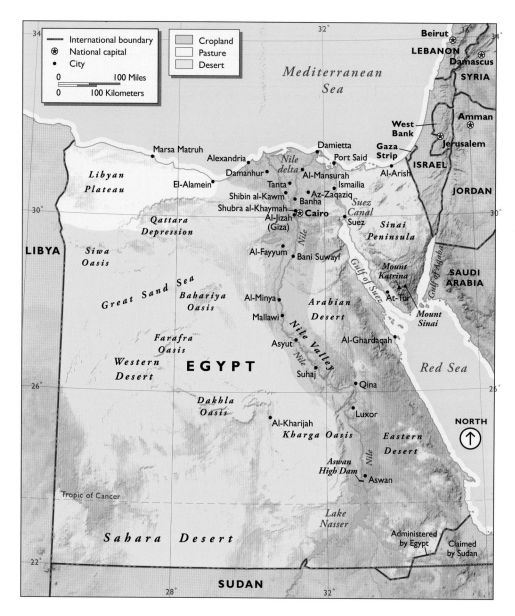

International boundary
National capital
City

Cropland
Pasture
Desert

0   100 Miles
0   100 Kilometers

Beirut
LEBANON
Damascus
SYRIA

Mediterranean
Sea

West
Bank
Amman
Gaza
Strip
Jerusalem
ISRAEL
JORDAN

Damietta
Marsa Matruh   Port Said
Alexandria   *Nile*   Al-Arish
delta
Damanhur   Al-Mansurah
Libyan   El-Alamein   Tanta   Ismailia
Plateau   Shibin al-Kawm   Az-Zaqaziq
Banha   *Suez*
Shubra al-Khaymah   *Canal*
Al-Jizah   **Cairo**
(Giza)   Suez
Qattara   *Sinai*
Depression   *Peninsula*

LIBYA
Siwa   Al-Fayyum   Bani Suwayf
Oasis

Mount
Great Sand Sea   *Katrina*
Bahariya   At-Tur   *Gulf of Aqaba*
Oasis   Al-Minya   *Arabian*   *Mount*   **SAUDI**
Mallawi   *Desert*   *Sinai*   **ARABIA**

Farafra
Oasis   Asyut
Western   Suhaj   *Nile Valley*   Al-Ghardaqah   *Red Sea*
Desert   **E G Y P T**
Qina

Dakhla
Oasis   Luxor   **NORTH**

Al-Kharijah
Kharga Oasis   *Eastern*
Desert

Aswan
High Dam   *Nile*
Aswan

Tropic of Cancer

Lake
Nasser
Sahara Desert   Administered   Claimed
by Egypt   by Sudan

SUDAN

Geography of Egypt

Mediterranean Sea. Where it meets the sea, it forms the rich, fertile Nile delta, which supports more than half of modern Egypt's agriculture. In ancient Egypt and still today, the Nile valley south of Cairo is referred to as Upper Egypt, and the Nile delta north of Cairo is referred to as Lower Egypt. Most Egyptians reside in the Nile valley and the Nile delta.

The Western Desert, a vast sandy plateau, comprises approximately two-thirds of Egypt's total land area, but only a tiny percentage of the population lives there. Some Egyptians live in the coastal towns along the Mediterranean shore, such as El-Alamein and Damietta, and others live in the five major oases: Bahariya, Dakhla, Farafra, Kharga, and Siwa. These oases, which are located in sunken areas and fed by springs, are all large enough to support agriculture and some communities. Dakhla Oasis is the largest of the five and also the longest

UPPER AND LOWER EGYPT

Most people think of north as up and south as down. However, Upper Egypt is in the southern region of the country and Lower Egypt is in the north. Ancient Egypt's southernmost border was at the site of the first cataract of the Nile River—a rocky area of steep river rapids just below the city of Aswan. The kingdom of Nubia lay to the south. Today, the border is located farther to the south, and the first cataract is the site of a huge dam, the Aswan High Dam, which is a crucial source of irrigation and electric power. Its construction also created Lake Nasser, which flooded much of what used to be Lower (northern) Nubia.

continually inhabited (since the Paleolithic period). The Western Desert also contains the lowest point in Egypt's topography, the Qattara Depression, which is 435 feet (133 m) below sea level.[6]

Unlike the Western Desert, the Eastern Desert is mostly rocky and mountainous. There are no oases in this desert, although there are some dry streambeds that can fill with water during rare times of rainfall. The Eastern Desert includes the Red Sea coast, some of which has been developed as resort areas for foreign and Egyptian tourists. The Eastern Desert is an important source of mineral deposits.

SIWA OASIS

The lush Siwa Oasis, covered with date and olive trees, is believed to have been inhabited since ancient times by the Berber people, who are indigenous to North Africa. The Berbers have their own language, culture, and handicrafts, which differ from those of other Egyptian peoples. However, the Berber people are Muslim and do share some cultural traits with other peoples.

In the seventh century BCE, a temple to the god Amun was built at the Siwa Oasis. Its oracle was considered so important that Alexander III visited it in 331 BCE to consult it and prove that he was the son of Amun.

The Western Desert covers approximately two-thirds of Egypt's land surface.

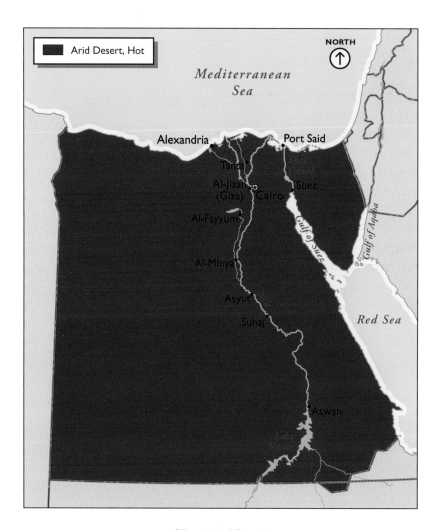

■	Arid Desert, Hot

NORTH ↑

Mediterranean Sea

Alexandria

Port Said

Tanta

Suez Canal

Al-Jizah (Giza)

Cairo

Suez

Al-Fayyum

Gulf of Suez

Gulf of Aqaba

Al-Minya

Asyut

Suhaj

Red Sea

Aswan

Lake Nasser

Climate of Egypt

AVERAGE TEMPERATURES AND RAINFALL

Region (City)	Average January Temperature Minimum/Maximum	Average July Temperature Minimum/Maximum	Average Rainfall January/July
Mediterranean Coastal Strip (Alexandria)	52/64°F (11/18°C)	73/84°F (23/29°C)	2/0 inches (5/0 cm)
Nile River Valley (Cairo)	46/64°F (8/18°C)	70/97°F (21/36°C)	0.2/0 inches (0.5/0 cm)
Southern Egypt (Aswan)	50/73°F (10/23°C)	79/106°F (26/41°C)	0/0 inches (0/0 cm)[7]

The Sinai Peninsula is a triangular wedge sandwiched between the African and Asian continents. It is separated from the Eastern Desert by the Suez Canal, which connects the Mediterranean and the Red Seas. The northern region of the peninsula is a flat limestone plateau, while the south is rocky and mountainous. Egypt's greatest petroleum deposits are found in this region, and it is also a source of minerals. In addition, many tourists come to this region to hike on Mount Sinai and Mount Katrina, to scuba dive and snorkel in the Red Sea, and to visit the national parks and protected areas.

CLIMATE

In general, Egypt's climate is hot and dry. The winter months are slightly cooler and have little to no rainfall, and the khamsin season in spring has hot winds and dust storms blowing in from the desert.

However, there is some regional variation. Along the Mediterranean coast, for example, there is more rainfall, the weather is cooler, and sea breezes make some days chilly. In the desert regions, there may be no rainfall all year; the days are much sunnier and hotter, although nighttime temperatures can drop drastically. In the mountains of Sinai, temperatures are lower and snow sometimes falls, even though it does not stick.

The Nile River has no tributaries in Egypt.

Oasis of Dakhla, Egypt

CHAPTER 3

ANIMALS AND NATURE: ANCIENT SYMBOLS

Many animals that can be found in Egypt today have been immortalized in the art of the ancient Egyptians. Cats are particularly iconic; both wild and domestic cats were sacred in ancient Egypt. Domestic cats were handy for keeping rats, mice, and snakes out of food stores, but they were also beloved pets. Cats were often depicted in paintings as part of the household. Bastet was a protective goddess with the head of a cat. Wild cats such as the desert lynx, the sand cat, and the Egyptian wildcat can be found in parts of Egypt today, as can domestic cats.

Another iconic animal of Egypt is the jackal. This wild canine, both predator and scavenger, could be seen lurking around cemeteries in ancient times. For this reason, the ancient Egyptians associated jackals

Cats, one of the iconic animals of Egypt, wander an empty street in a Coptic area of Cairo.

In Egyptian cuisine, pigeons are considered a delicacy.

with death and gave a jackal's head to Anubis, the god of death and embalming who watched over the mummification process. Jackals still lurk around Egypt today, although they are not likely found in modern cemeteries.

Several birds also have been associated with ancient Egyptian gods. Horus, the son of gods Isis and Osiris, had the head of a falcon. The falcon was also associated with Re, the sun god. Today, several types of falcons can be found in Egypt, including red-footed falcons, peregrine falcons, and sooty falcons. The ibis was associated with the god Thoth, who had the head of an ibis. Thoth was the divine scribe and inventor of numbers, and the Egyptians believe he gave them their hieroglyphic writing system. This elegant, long-legged wading bird used to be seen along the shores of the Nile but is now endangered.

DOMESTIC ANIMALS

The early Egyptians domesticated cattle and kept them for meat, milk, leather, horns, and labor. They were often depicted on tomb walls in scenes of daily life, but they were also sacred symbols. Hathor, the goddess of love and joy, appeared in various forms as a cow, a cow-headed woman, a woman with cow ears, and a woman with horns. Bulls were associated with masculinity and with the pharaoh.

A scroll shows the images of Egyptian gods Anubis, who had the head of a jackal, and Horus, with the head of a falcon.

The ancient Egyptians also domesticated sheep. These animals were used not only for their meat, milk, skins, and wool but also to trample seed into the fields to assist with planting crops. The ram was associated with fertility and with the creator gods Khnum and Amun. Mummified rams have been found in tomb sites, complete with golden masks.

A camel can survive four to seven days in severe heat without drinking water.

Horses were introduced to Egypt between 1600 and 1500 BCE, along with the chariot, and became important both in peace and in war. Before Egyptians had horses, they primarily used boats for transporting goods on the Nile and donkeys for transporting goods on land. Today, Egyptian Arabian horses hold a prestigious place in equestrian circles.

DESERT SYMBOLS

Ancient Egyptians had a healthy respect for the cobra, which was usually depicted rearing up, hood spread, ready to strike. Given the power of this dangerous reptile, it was associated with royalty and often adorned the crowns of pharaohs. The cobra was also a symbol of Lower Egypt, represented by the goddess Wadjet. Several varieties of cobra can still be found in Egypt today, the most famous of which is the Egyptian cobra.

A white camel rests near the Pyramids of Giza.

The scorpion is a poisonous arachnid, or spider, of the desert. It is associated with the goddess Selket, who was a protector of the dead and had healing powers, especially against scorpion bites and snakebites. She wore a scorpion on top of her head. A golden statue of this goddess was found in the famous tomb of Tutankhamen. The goddess Isis was also believed to have power over scorpions and to heal persons stung by them, as described in the myth of Isis and the seven scorpions.

The scarab is a dung beetle. Its form was used on amulets to protect the wearer from evil, and large heart scarab amulets engraved with words from the Book of the Dead were found on important mummies. Egyptians associated the scarab with the morning sun and with rebirth or miraculous birth. The god Khepri—a god of creation, the movement of the sun, and of rebirth—is therefore associated with

THE TWO LADIES OF EGYPT

The Two Ladies of Egypt, or Nebti, were two goddesses who were believed to protect the pharaoh. One was the goddess Wadjet, who was represented by a cobra and the symbol of Lower Egypt. The other was the goddess Nekhbet, the vulture and symbol of Upper Egypt. Together, they represented a unified Egypt under one king. Traditionally, the pharaoh would receive a Nebti name, such as "He of the two ladies," as part of his official title.

A cobra, one of the symbols of Lower Egypt, rears up, ready to strike.

PAPYRUS

The word *papyrus* comes from the Greek word *papyros,* from which the English word "paper" is derived. *Papyrus* refers to both the plant that grows along the Nile and the paper that is made from it. It can also refer to a specific papyrus document.

Papyrus was made by removing the outer layer of a freshly picked reed and cutting the pith, or center, into thin strips. One layer of strips was laid side by side, and another layer was laid crosswise on top of it. Then, the combined layers were pounded for a long time with a mallet. The secretions from the plant, along with the pounding, were enough to hold the sheet together.

Several sheets of papyrus would be glued together to form a long scroll. The papyrus scroll was the ancient Egyptian version of the book, and scribes kept libraries of them.

the scarab and appears as a man with the head of a scarab beetle.

EGYPTIAN PLANTS

A number of common plants are traditionally identified with Egypt because of its history, landscape, and culture. Perhaps the most iconic plant of Egypt is the papyrus, a reed that used to grow abundantly along the shores of the Nile. The ancient Egyptians famously used it to make writing scrolls, but they also bound the reeds together to build boats and to make sandals. Papyrus had vanished

Date palm trees are common along the Nile River and in oases.

from Egypt by the nineteenth century but was reintroduced in 1872 with plants from France. It is now cultivated in small plots, mainly for the purpose of making souvenir papyrus scrolls and decorations for tourists.

The date palm and the doum palm are two common fruit-bearing palm trees found in Egyptian oases. The flavor of the doum palm fruit has been compared to that of gingerbread. Another fruit-bearing tree grown in Egypt is the fig, a common Mediterranean tree. Both the common fig and the sycamore fig are found in Egypt.

Henna is another plant native to Egypt. Its leaves are dried and ground into a powder that is used to dye and condition hair and to paint the hands of a bride before her wedding. The powder itself is green, but the resulting color is reddish-orange.

> The Egyptians mummified animals as well as people.

ENDANGERED SPECIES AND PROTECTED LANDS

Today, some of the species in Egypt are threatened by habitat destruction due to development and desertification, hunting and exploitation, and pollution. Ten species of reptiles are considered endangered, including the green turtle, a rare sea turtle that nests and feeds in the sea grasses off the Mediterranean coast. Also critically endangered is the Egyptian tortoise, a tiny desert-dwelling creature found in Egypt and Libya. This little tortoise has been heavily exploited in the pet trade and may even be extinct in Egypt. The hammerhead shark is another endangered sea creature found off Egypt's Mediterranean coast. In the Red Sea, the coral reef ecosystem is threatened by oil spills and other pollution.

Approximately ten bird species are endangered, including the Egyptian vulture. In ancient times, the vulture was the symbol of Upper Egypt and associated with the goddess Nekhbet. It is estimated that 17 mammal species are endangered, among them the Nubian ibex of the Eastern Desert and the Barbary sheep of the Western Desert.

ENDANGERED SPECIES IN EGYPT

According to the International Union for Conservation of Nature (IUCN), Egypt is home to the following numbers of species that are categorized by the organization as Critically Endangered, Endangered, or Vulnerable:

Mammals	17
Birds	10
Reptiles	10
Amphibians	0
Fishes	35
Mollusks	0
Other Invertebrates	46
Plants	2
Total	120[1]

SAINT CATHERINE PROTECTORATE

The Saint Catherine Protectorate in South Sinai seeks to preserve natural, historical, architectural, and cultural heritage. It is a mountainous desert region that includes Mount Katrina, which is the highest point in Egypt at 8,625 feet (2,629 m) above sea level, and a town by the same name.[3]

The region is home to a variety of wildlife, including many resident and migratory birds, foxes, ibexes, hyraxes, and the world's smallest butterfly: the Sinai Baton Blue Butterfly. It is also the site of a sixth-century Byzantine monastery—the oldest continually inhabited monastery in the world—which contains a fourth-century Byzantine church. In addition, it is the site of Mount Sinai (Jabal Musa, or "The Mountain of Moses," in Arabic), which is considered holy in Islam, Christianity, and Judaism.

The traditional people of the region are the Jebaliya Bedouin, whom Byzantine Emperor Justinian I sent to the area in the sixth century to protect the monastery. Originally Christian, the Jebaliya later converted to Islam. Unlike many other Bedouin tribes, who are nomadic desert dwellers, the Jebaliya (whose name means "of the mountains") live in the mountainous regions around the wadis of Saint Catherine and are expert gardeners. A visitor's center and museum in the Saint Catherine Protectorate features an exhibit on the culture and history of the Bedouin people in the region.

The Egyptian government has developed programs to protect the nation's vulnerable areas and biodiversity. In 1992, Egypt ratified the international Convention on Biological Diversity at the Rio Earth Summit. Then in 1998, Egypt enacted the National Biodiversity Strategy Action Plan. The major goals of both programs are to implement strategies to research and protect animal and plant species and their habitats and to promote responsibility and sustainable practices.

Egypt has 29 national protected areas, which cover 15 percent of the nation's territory.[2] They are divided into four categories: coastal, wetlands, desert, and geologic. This last set includes the Petrified Forest, the remains of a 35-million-year-old wood in the greater Cairo area.

CHAPTER 4

HISTORY: WHERE CIVILIZATION BEGAN

People have been living in the territory that is now Egypt since Paleolithic times. Approximately 10,000 years ago, after the last Ice Age, Egypt was a lush and grassy land. The apparent remains of Neolithic settlements dating as far back as 7500 BCE have been found in the Nabta Playa basin in the south of the country. Evidence of pottery, grain, and hunting has been found in the area.

With time, the land began drying up. People in the region adapted to the increasing scarcity of food sources and began forming settlements. The oldest village discovered in Egypt dates from between 5000 and 4000 BCE. The people developed agricultural practices, growing wheat and barley and domesticating cattle, goats, and sheep. They also built furniture, wove linen cloth from flax, made pottery, crafted metal objects, made and sailed in boats, fished, baked bread, and brewed beer. The people

The Great Pyramid of Giza was constructed for Pharaoh Khufu.

MUMMIFICATION

Ancient Egyptians believed that the body needed to be preserved for the soul to reach the afterlife. Specially trained priests embalmed the bodies of kings and queens. First, the body was washed. Then, the lungs, liver, stomach, and intestines were removed. The heart was left in, because Egyptians believed it would be judged before the person entered the afterlife. However, the brain was not considered important. It was pulled out through the nose with a hook and then discarded. Resin was sometimes inserted into the head to keep it from collapsing.

Next, the body was covered and filled with a sodium carbonate mineral called natron to dry it out. Forty days later, the body was washed again, anointed with oil, and wrapped in strips of linen. Amulets and verses from the Book of the Dead were placed with the body for protection. Several more layers of linen and cloth were added before the body was placed into two coffins and then a large sarcophagus. After the funeral rituals, the body would be placed in its tomb with all the objects the person would need in the afterlife.

in this region traded with people in Asia and possibly Sumeria.

Many ancient settlements have been found, demonstrating that the ancient Egyptian people of this period gradually developed advanced irrigation techniques, the making of papyrus paper, hieroglyphic writing, increasingly sophisticated arts, religious cults, and complex sociopolitical systems that became cities. By the end of the fourth millennium BCE, several city-states had been established and two kingdoms had emerged: one in Upper Egypt and one in Lower Egypt.

DYNASTIC (PHARAONIC) EGYPT

During the Early Dynastic period (circa 3100–2686 BCE), Upper and Lower Egypt came together as a unified country, and ancient Egyptian religion and culture began taking shape. The Egyptians developed a complex order of gods and the concept of a divine kingship. They also had a strong belief in the afterlife and developed the process of mummification and the building of large tombs for the nobility. The first king of this period, Menes, established as Egypt's capital the city of Memphis, approximately 12 miles (19 km) south of modern Cairo.

The Old Kingdom (2686–2181 BCE) was most characterized by the construction of massive pyramids as tombs for the pharaohs. During the Middle Kingdom period (circa 2181–1750 BCE), Egypt flourished in foreign relations, military actions, architecture, the arts, and literature. Advances in trade and migration brought Egypt in contact with many lands in the Near East. Egypt came to control parts of Nubia and received slaves and precious materials, such as gold and copper.

During the Second Intermediate period (circa 1640–1550 BCE), Egypt was once again divided. It had fallen partly under the rule of a Semitic people called the Hyksos, who had come from Asia, occupied northern Egypt, and gained control of the country. The Hyksos introduced many new things to Egypt, including the horse, the chariot, body armor, and the lute. However, the Egyptians resented the presence of the Hyksos.

In ancient Egypt, young children did not wear clothing.

NOTABLE PHARAOHS OF THE NEW KINGDOM

During the New Kingdom period (circa 1550–1069 BCE), Ancient Egypt was prosperous and powerful. Several of the notable pharaohs from this time included:

Hatshepsut was the third female pharaoh known to historians. She ruled for 22 years, reaching out to foreign lands and acquiring great wealth and power.

Thutmose III was Hatshepsut's stepson. He raised a great army and expanded the empire by defeating a coalition of princes in Palestine.

Akhenaten broke tradition by establishing a monotheistic cult to the god Aten, the sun disk. He and his queen Nefertiti moved the capital from Thebes to Tell el-Almarna and supported a new style of sensual, real-world art.

Tutankhamen became king at age nine and died at 18. He restored Thebes as the capital and Amun as the principal god. He became famous after treasures were discovered in his tomb in 1922.

Meanwhile, to the south, a new threat was arising: The kingdom of Kush in Nubia was gaining power. The king of Thebes, Seqenenre, raised an army against the Hyksos and was killed in battle. His son, Kamose, the king of Thebes, hoped to avenge his father and regain control over Egypt, but he, too, was killed. His brother, Ahmose I, was left to carry out their father's will.

THE NEW KINGDOM

It was during the New Kingdom period (circa 1550–1069 BCE) that Egypt consolidated and built its power and influence, becoming one of the first great empires of the ancient world. Ahmose I succeeded in driving out the Hyksos and regaining the title of pharaoh.

The mask of King Tutankhamen was discovered in his tomb in 1922.

He then led a successful campaign to conquer Nubia, which became an essential supplier of gold—gold that would fill the pharaoh's coffers and help build a rich and powerful kingdom.

During this period, the Egyptians pressed into the Middle East and absorbed many city-states into their growing territory. By 1390 BCE, Egypt was a sprawling, prosperous empire in its Golden Age and widely respected by its subjects and neighbors. Amenhotep III perfected the art of diplomacy during his reign, relying on his vast supplies of gold from Nubia to maintain influence over the kings of neighboring lands, such as Babylonia and Assyria.

By approximately 1000 BCE, Egypt's greatness had begun decaying. A group of unknown origin, known only as the Sea Peoples, attacked Egypt and conquered neighboring kingdoms. Egypt lost its territories in Asia and then in Nubia. People desperate to pay their burdensome taxes robbed the tombs of the buried pharaohs. The nation itself began splitting up, and there was no strong center of power. In 728 BCE, kings from Nubia invaded and established a dynasty of Nubian rule. Then, Egypt was invaded by the Assyrians from the east. Egypt had some success in regaining control over Nubia and launching military campaigns in the Near East, but it soon faced a new rival: the mighty Persian Empire.

The pharaoh Ramses II had five wives.

PERSIAN, MACEDONIAN, AND ROMAN/ BYZANTINE RULE

Cyrus II of Persia had created the biggest, most powerful empire the world had ever seen. In 525 BCE, his son Cambyses II invaded Egypt and established a Persian dynasty. Egyptian revolts succeeded in ridding the country of Persian control and restoring a native dynasty. But the Persians came back with a vengeance, installing a new dynasty in 343 BCE and ruling oppressively over the Egyptians, who hated them.

Meanwhile, Alexander III, king of Macedonia, was intent on establishing an empire of his own. His army defeated the Persians in Asia Minor and in Syria, and when he arrived in Egypt in 332 BCE, he had little trouble overthrowing the Persian rulers. The Egyptians welcomed him as a hero. Soon after his arrival, he commissioned the construction of a new port city, Alexandria, which would be a strategic commercial and political center. It would later develop into the cultural and intellectual center of the Western world.

Alexander III respected the Egyptian culture and religion and even claimed to be the son of Amun. He was revered by the Egyptians as a god and a true pharaoh and was mummified upon his death in 323 BCE. After Alexander died, his childhood friend Ptolemy took control. Ptolemy founded the Ptolemaic dynasty, a 300-year succession of Greek-speaking, Macedonian pharaohs.

The last was Cleopatra, one of the most well-known rulers of Egypt. She had a love affair with Roman ruler Gaius Julius Caesar and later

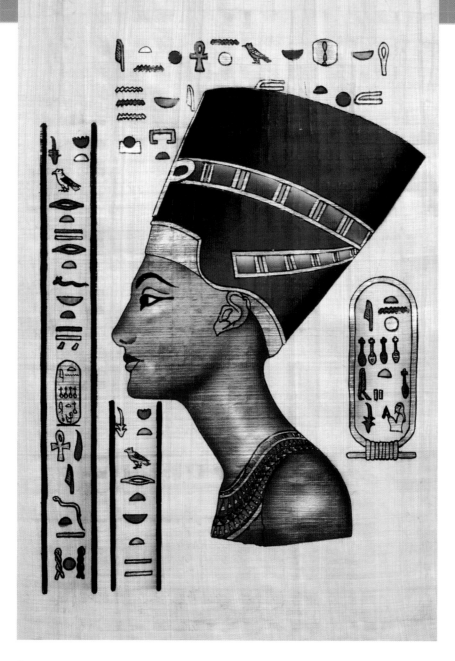

A papyrus contains a portrait of Cleopatra.

married Roman general Mark Antony, who stood to challenge Caesar's heir, Augustus. In 30 BCE, after Roman forces led by Augustus defeated Egyptian forces led by Antony at the Battle of Actium, Rome was able to take control of the country. This defeat led Antony and Cleopatra to commit suicide.

As a province of the Roman Empire, Egypt was under tight political control. Egyptians had to pay high taxes to the Romans, and the country became a major supplier of grain and agricultural products for the empire. Culturally, the traditional Egyptian style of art gave way to Greek and Roman styles.

Cleopatra's story has been told many times, including by William Shakespeare in the play *Antony and Cleopatra*.

Christianity arrived in Egypt during the first century CE and found many converts. However, Christians were frequently harassed or persecuted until 313 CE, when the Emperor Constantine I issued the Edict of Milan, establishing religious tolerance throughout the empire. In 330 CE, Constantine established a new capital city in Byzantium, beginning the transition into a Christian Byzantine Empire.

ARAB CONQUEST

In the early seventh century, Islam appeared as a new religion in Arabia. Between 640 and 642, Arabs swept into Egypt, defeating the Byzantines near the Egyptian city of Babylon and taking control. There, they built a new capital, Al-Fustat, the remains of which can now be seen in Old

Cairo. The Arabic language and the Sunni Islamic religion gradually took hold. The new Arab rulers did not force their new subjects to convert to Islam, but those who did received special treatment.

For 200 years, governors appointed by caliphs in Damascus and then Baghdad ruled Egypt. In 868, local dynasties took over. Following a famine, the Shiite Fatimid caliphate stepped in from Tunisia and established a dynasty that ruled until 1171. As Shiites, this caliphate followed a different branch of Islam than the Sunnis. This caliphate established Cairo as the new capital city. The great Kurdish warrior Saladin arrived in Egypt in 1169 and seized power, restoring Sunni Islam to Egypt. His successors in Egypt were known as the Ayyubid dynasty.

The Ayyubid rulers fortified their armies with young Turkish slaves whom they raised, converted to Islam, and trained as warriors. These slaves were known as the Mamluks. Technically, they were to be freed after their military training, but they were still required to serve in the army of the sultan.

In 1250, the Mamluks seized power from the Ayyubid rulers. Under the Mamluks, the nation's commerce thrived. Its location made it a crucial

SALADIN

Saladin is considered a great hero in Arab Muslim history. He helped build an Islamic empire that stretched across the Middle East and northern Africa. He became famous for fighting and defeating the Frank Crusader armies at Hittin, in Palestine in 1187, which allowed him to conquer most of the Kingdom of Jerusalem.

passageway between Europe and the Far East, and the Mamluks controlled important trade routes. However, by the end of the fifteenth century, the Mamluks' power was waning. Egypt's population and economy had been seriously marred by the bubonic plague. At the same time, the Mamluks had lost control over trade routes, as European explorers discovered new ways to reach East Africa and Asia by sea.

The ancient Egyptians were responsible for many inventions, including toothbrushes, plows, and cement.

Meanwhile, the Ottoman Empire was steadily growing. In 1516, the Ottomans struck the Mamluk Empire, first overtaking Syria and then Egypt in 1517. The Ottomans imposed new laws and new taxes on the Egyptians and required them to pay tribute to the empire. But for the most part, the Mamluks remained in local administrative control while the Ottomans ruled out of Istanbul.

Under the Ottoman Empire, Egypt continued to be a successful exporter of textiles, coffee, sugar, and rice. However, most of its revenues were going to the Ottoman sultan. Also, peasants were being severely exploited by tax farmers, who collected revenues on agricultural products and sent them to the Ottoman sultan, pocketing as much as possible.

During the eighteenth century, Egypt began experiencing an economic and political decline. The country was losing prominence as an exporter to Europe, as European nations began importing from the Americas and other parts of the world. Internal political strife further stressed the economy, and by the end of the eighteenth century, many Egyptians were starving.

Three mummies are shown on display at the Egyptian Funerary Arts Gallery at the Museum of Fine Arts in Boston.

FRENCH AND BRITISH CONTROL

The French and the English had long been in conflict, especially in their efforts to establish colonial control over other nations. In 1798, Napoléon I launched a campaign to take control of Egypt. In doing so, he hoped to strike indirectly at Great Britain by cutting off its main passageway to India, a key British colony. Napoléon I also imagined himself establishing a new French Empire that stretched all the way to India. He overtook the Mamluk army in Alexandria and pushed his way into Egypt, but his troops suffered from the climate and terrain, and his rule was not welcome by the Egyptians. He was ultimately thwarted by a joint English and Ottoman force, which defeated the French troops in 1801.

Muhammad 'Ali, called the father of modern Egypt, was of Turkish-Albanian origin. He landed in Egypt with a regiment of Albanian soldiers sent by the Ottomans in 1801 to fight

THE ROSETTA STONE

A French soldier discovered the Rosetta Stone, an ancient stone tablet, in July 1799. It dates back to the rule of Ptolemy V in the second century BCE and is engraved in three languages: Greek, hieroglyphic, and demotic. Until discovery of the Rosetta Stone, no one had been able to decipher the hieroglyphic language. But having the three languages side by side (along with the fact that Greek was a known language) provided the key to breaking the code. Several scholars worked to decipher the hieroglyphs from the stone, but Jean François Champollion made the most progress.

the French. He remained in Egypt and gained the support of the local *ulama* (the educated Muslim elite, who acted as community leaders and educators). By 1805, he had convinced the Ottoman sultan to appoint him viceroy. Six years later, in a bold maneuver, he invited all the Mamluks to a ceremony in Cairo, after which his men murdered them. Those who escaped were killed later.

Muhammad 'Ali made many reforms that transformed and modernized society. He got rid of the tax farming system but brought most of Egypt's land under government control, collecting taxes to finance his reforms. He developed new irrigation techniques, reclaimed desert lands for agriculture, and introduced cash crops such as cotton and tobacco. He increased the size of the army, drafting and training Egyptian peasants to fill the ranks. He also worked to develop higher education and created a government press, which issued books and newspapers. In addition, he worked to modernize medicine, establishing new hospitals, a school for midwives, and public health programs including vaccination against smallpox. All of these achievements laid the foundations for a strong, educated, trained class of native Egyptian citizens.

Egyptian writer Naguib Mahfouz won the Nobel Prize for Literature in 1988.

In 1839, Muhammad 'Ali felt so powerful that he challenged the Ottoman sultan for autonomous control of Egypt and Syria. His son

Muhammad 'Ali is known as the father of modern Egypt.

Ibrahim Pasha crushed the Ottomans in the Battle of Nezib, just north of the modern border between Turkey and Syria, bringing about their surrender. However, the British feared the collapse of the Ottoman Empire and did not trust Muhammad 'Ali. They did not want to lose access to India via the Middle East, nor did they want the Russians to gain control of Eastern Europe if the Ottomans turned to Russia for help. So, the British intervened, and a coalition of European powers forced Muhammad 'Ali to retreat. However, they agreed to recognize him as the ruler of Egypt and granted Egypt autonomy, although it remained nominally part of the Ottoman Empire.

Muhammad 'Ali's successors continued with modernizing reforms but under increasing European influence. In 1851, England began building a rail line connecting Alexandria to Cairo. In 1859, work began on the Suez Canal, backed by the French and international investors and produced by forced labor by Egyptian peasants under terrible conditions.

SUEZ CANAL

The Suez Canal, which connects the Mediterranean Sea at Port Said to the Red Sea at Suez, is one of the most important and most heavily used waterways in the world. The canal provides the fastest shipping route between Europe and the Indian Ocean, and it also connects Europe to the oil-rich Gulf nations. Therefore, the Suez Canal has had enormous political and economic importance since its conception. Digging began in 1859, and the canal opened for navigation ten years later. Egyptian peasants performed most of the labor, toiling in poor conditions and for little pay. Begun as a joint French-Egyptian venture, Egypt gained full control of the canal in 1956.

Under Isma'il Pasha, Muhammad 'Ali's grandson, Egypt experienced a brief economic boom, as the American Civil War forced Europe to buy its cotton from Egypt. But Isma'il began borrowing foreign funds to invest in numerous projects, including schools, cultural institutions, infrastructure, and industrial advancements.

Later in Isma'il's reign, as cotton prices dropped, he found himself deeply in debt. In 1878, England and France, the major investors in Egypt, stepped in and established control over Egypt's treasury. Isma'il tried to get rid of them and to draft a new constitution, but England and France removed him from power and installed his son, whom they easily controlled.

Egyptian women have had the right to vote since 1956.

In 1881 a group of army officers led by 'Urabi Pasha raised a nationalist movement against the French and British. When France and Great Britain sent naval fleets to Alexandria in response, riots broke out in the city. The French fleet turned around and sailed home, leaving the British alone. They bombarded the city, which only strengthened the commitment of the nationalists. On September 13, 1882, the British confronted and defeated the nationalist army at Tell el-Kebir, and 'Urabi was arrested and exiled. The British had taken military control of Egypt.

Despite England's earlier promise to withdraw its troops, it refused to leave Egypt. The nationalist movement was transformed into the Nationalist Party, and many rival parties emerged, each publishing its own newspaper. The British took steps to curb the influence of the Nationalist

Party. In 1914, when World War I broke out and the Ottoman Empire sided with Germany, England cut ties with the Ottomans and declared a protectorate over Egypt. This meant that the English secured the country with military forces and maintained partial control over Egypt's government.

THE 1919 REVOLUTION

After World War I, a native Egyptian lawyer named Saʻd Zaghlul emerged as a leader and spokesman of the opposition to British rule. Unrest spread through the country after Britain refused to negotiate with Egypt, and Egypt was not invited to the 1919 Paris Peace Conference, where the nation's leaders had hoped to present their case for independence.

Britain responded in March 1919 by exiling Zaghlul and his colleagues, but this made things worse. Riots broke out. Both Copts and Muslims stood together in solidarity, and both men and women participated in the protests. Great Britain managed to control the revolt, but it was clear that Egypt would no longer accept foreign rule. In 1922, Britain formally declared the end of the protectorate, although it imposed certain conditions. Britain would retain control of the Suez Canal, for example, along with other business interests. Furthermore, Egypt would be required to go to war if need be to protect British interests in Egypt.

The national anthem is "Bilady, Bilady, Bilady." *Bilady* means "my homeland" in Arabic.

Uplifted by hope and moved by nationalist pride, Egyptians drafted a new constitution for themselves. In 1923, Zaghlul and his companions were allowed to return, and Egypt held elections for its first parliament. Meanwhile, Egypt was experiencing a cultural and intellectual boom. Many great authors and thinkers rose to prominence; books, magazines, and newspapers abounded; the great Umm Kulthum emerged from humble origins and launched the longest, most influential career of any Egyptian singer; Radio Cairo began broadcasting; and a new film industry emerged.

In 1936, Farouk I, the great-great grandson of Muhammad 'Ali, ascended to the throne. He was popular among the Egyptian people at first, but by the end of the 1940s, they were dissatisfied again. Corruption and dissent plagued the government, and King Farouk proved to be incompetent. In 1948, a failed campaign against Israel in Palestine further demoralized the people. Another issue was that the British still had strong political and economic influence on the country. Strikes and protests broke out, and on Black Saturday—January 26, 1952—angry mobs burned the Westernized downtown Cairo.

THE 1952 REVOLUTION

On July 23, 1952, 300 officers took control of the government in a coup. They called themselves the Free Officers and were led by Gamal Abdel Nasser. In 1954, Nasser established himself as Egypt's new leader. Instead of securing democracy, he crushed his opposition and put in place a one-party system. He became popular for his pro-Arab and anti-West stances.

Gamal Abdel Nasser, 1954

Nasser instituted a policy of socialism and Arab nationalism. As part of this policy, Nasser made sweeping agricultural land redistribution reforms that improved the lives of many lower-class citizens. He nationalized all private banks and many private companies, including international companies. The most prominent of these was the Suez Canal Company. Reclaiming the Suez revenues was a big boon for Egypt and a big blow to England and France, who along with Israel had attempted to retake it in a short-lived and unsuccessful attack in 1956. Nasser also built the Aswan High Dam, which ended the annual flooding of the Nile and created Lake Nasser, displacing a large number of Egypt's Nubian population.

In 1967, Nasser plotted with Syria to move against Israel in what they saw as Palestinian territory. To their surprise, Israel launched a preemptive strike on Egypt, wiping out the nation's entire air force and seizing control of the Gaza Strip and Sinai Peninsula. The 1967 war shook Nasser; he resigned from office but later reinstated himself after a popular outcry. He died on September 28, 1970, and his vice president, Anwar el-Sadat, took office.

Sadat abandoned the socialist policies of Nasser and opened up the economy to private and foreign investors. He continued military campaigns against Israel to regain the territories they had occupied in 1967. The most significant and successful of these was the 1973 War, also known as the October War, in which Egyptian troops crossed the Suez Canal and launched a surprise attack on Israeli troops in the Sinai Peninsula. The Egyptians broke through Israeli defenses and advanced into the Sinai, but the Israelis ultimately defeated them, and a cease-fire was brokered by the United Nations. Despite their failure to regain the Sinai, the maneuver was seen as a huge victory by the Egyptian people, who still commemorate the event as a national holiday on October 6. In the end, Sadat gained victory only through diplomacy. In 1979, he signed a peace treaty with Israeli leader Menachem Begin, which had been brokered a year earlier by the United States in the Camp David Peace Accords.

Hosni Mubarak survived at least six assassination attempts.

Between 1979 and 1982, Israel withdrew from the Sinai and the land was restored to Egypt. On October 6, 1981, Islamic extremists opposed to the peace treaty assassinated Sadat, and Hosni Mubarak, his vice president, took office. Egypt was finally free from foreign rule but not from the authoritarian rule of its own leaders.

President Anwar el-Sadat, *right*, and Vice President Hosni Mubarak watch
a military parade in 1981, shortly before Sadat was assassinated.

CHAPTER 5
PEOPLE:
MODERN EGYPTIANS

Egypt has a rapidly growing population, from 62.3 million in 1995 to 80.5 million in 2010 and a projected 95.6 million by 2026. Approximately 43 percent of Egyptians live in urban areas.[1]

Population growth has put a strain on already overcrowded Cairo and poses a challenge to the country as a whole, with its limited natural resources, sources of freshwater, and habitable, arable land. Population growth also puts a strain on the nation's educational system and other public services, which are already strained by a struggling economy.

Recent family planning programs launched by the government and other organizations have had only limited

Approximately one-quarter of the Arab world's population lives in Egypt.

An Egyptian woman takes a break from selling trinkets to tourists at the Sphinx outside Cairo.

success, due to Egyptians' religious beliefs, tendency toward early marriage, and traditional inclination toward large families, especially in poor and rural communities. However, trends seem to show the fertility rate going down.[2]

ETHNIC AND RELIGIOUS GROUPS

For thousands of years, Egypt has occupied a key location as a link among Africa, the Middle East and Asia, and Europe. It has been a trade and migration route, was a great conqueror when pharaohs were in power, and has been conquered many times since the sixth century BCE.

Consequently, modern Egyptians are an ethnic blend, descendants of the ancient Egyptian people of northeast Africa and a mix of the many other ethnicities that have passed through and been adopted into society. These ethnicities have included, for example, Nubian, Libyan, Bedouin, Berber, Persian, Roman, Greek, Arab, Turkish, and Circassian. In a 2006 census, 99.6 percent

DEMOGRAPHICS

Age structure:
   0–14 years: 33 %
   15–64 years: 62.8 %
   65 years and over: 4.5% (2011 estimate)

Life expectancy:
   Total population: 72.6 years
   Male: 70.07 years
   Female: 75.38 years[3]

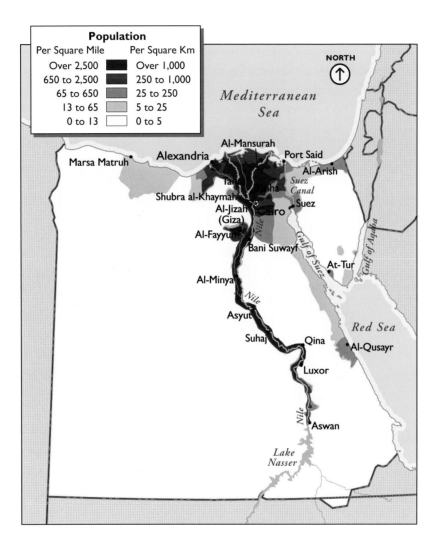

Population

Per Square Mile		Per Square Km
Over 2,500		Over 1,000
650 to 2,500		250 to 1,000
65 to 650		25 to 250
13 to 65		5 to 25
0 to 13		0 to 5

NORTH

Mediterranean Sea

Marsa Matruh

Alexandria

Al-Mansurah

Port Said

Al-Arish

Suez Canal

Shubra al-Khaymah

Al-Jizah (Giza)

Cairo

Suez

Al-Fayyum

Bani Suwayf

Gulf of Suez

Gulf of Aqaba

At-Tur

Al-Minya

Nile

Asyut

Red Sea

Suhaj

Qina

Al-Qusayr

Luxor

Nile

Aswan

Lake Nasser

Population Density of Egypt

of the population identified themselves as ethnically Egyptian, and only 0.4 percent as "other."[4] Ethnic minorities include non-Arab Nubians; dark-skinned people of southern Egypt and northern Sudan, who have their own language; the nomadic desert-dwelling Bedouins in the Sinai Peninsula, who consider themselves ancestrally Arab in origin; and the Berber people, who inhabit the Siwa Oasis.

Egypt is an Islamic country, with 90 percent of the population identifying themselves as Muslim, mostly Sunni.[5] There is also a Coptic Christian minority. It has existed in Egypt since the early days of Christianity, when Egypt was part of the Roman and then Byzantine Empires, and before the arrival of Arab Muslims in the seventh century.

SUFISM

Sufism is a form of Islamic mysticism that emphasizes direct communion with God through love and devotion. Sufis use music, chanting, and dance in their rituals, often achieving trancelike states. Sufism is popular in Egypt. Sufis are associated with the whirling dervish dance, which has its origins in Sufi tradition. Most performances of the dance, however, are actually done by entertainers and not Sufi practitioners.

In Egypt, Islam has traditionally been of a moderate, tolerant variety, although several incidents of terrorist activity have occurred over the years. Most Egyptians do not subscribe to extremism, and in part, because so many rely on tourism for their livelihood, many strongly oppose terrorism. Until the creation of Israel in 1948 and the ensuing tensions

An Egyptian man prays while reading from a Christian
text at the Coptic Hanging Church in Cairo.

MUSLIM-COPT CONFLICT

On New Year's Eve, 2010, a suicide bomber attacked Two Saints Church in Alexandria, killing 23 Coptic Christians. Then on January 11, 2011, a former police officer shot and killed a man and wounded five more, all Coptic Christians, on a train in Samalout. Some worry that this is part of a rising trend of conflict between Muslims and Christians, as has been developing in other parts of the Middle East. But former United Nations Secretary General Boutros Boutros-Ghali, himself an Egyptian Copt, does not agree:

> Our ties are far too old to be destroyed. Copts and Muslims have lived together in Egypt for 14 centuries. There have always been highs and lows between the religious groups, but never collective hate toward one another. I'm actually far more inclined to believe that the massacre in Alexandria will strengthen our bonds.... The attack in Alexandria was meant to foment unrest; it was meant to destabilize Egypt. If the entire world starts talking about a conflict between Copts and Muslims, it will divide our country.[6]

and conflicts with Egypt and the Muslim Arab world, a small Jewish Egyptian population had coexisted relatively peacefully for centuries alongside Egyptian Christians and Muslims.

Unfortunately, Coptic Christians have been the targets of periodic violence in Alexandria and southern Egypt since the 1990s, spurring vigorous protests by Copts for more protection from the government. Indeed, since 2000, there have been several incidents of sectarian violence and evidence of increased radicalization among Copts and Muslims. Despite this tension, however, many Egyptian Muslims and Copts pride themselves on their long-standing peaceful ties.

Interior of an Islamic mosque in Alexandria

YOU SAY IT!

English	Egyptian Arabic
Hello	Ahlan (AH-len)
Good-bye	Ma'is salaama (ma-ah sa-LAH-ma)
Thank you	Shukran (SHUK-run)
You're welcome	'Afwan (AF-wan)

LANGUAGE

The official language of Egypt is Arabic. Unlike many other languages, including English, Arabic has two different forms: Standard (or Classical) Arabic and regional dialects.

Standard Arabic is the written form and the form used in official documents, classical literature, newspapers, and religious rites. It is the language of the Koran and is the same throughout all Arabic-speaking countries. Standard Arabic is considered a more sophisticated form of expression, with complex grammatical rules. It must be learned in school, as it is not spoken at home. Therefore, uneducated people often do not learn it, except in the context of religious studies.

Regional dialects are what Arabic speakers learn at home and commonly speak with each other. The dialects differ from country to country, and in many cases, Arabic speakers from one country find it difficult to understand the dialect of another country. Because Egypt has

Egyptian documents show hieroglyphic and Arabic writing.

HIEROGLYPHS

Hieroglyphic script is a beautiful, complex system of writing consisting of symbols that represent sounds or concepts. Hieroglyphics is the writing painted or inscribed on temple walls and monuments.

Hieratic script developed around the same time and provided a simplified way of writing hieroglyphics quickly on papyrus. This was more practical for priests and scribes in day-to-day record keeping, storytelling, and correspondence. Demotic script evolved much later. It provided an even simpler and faster way of handwriting the hieratic symbols and only very distantly resembles the original hieroglyphs.

Despite the development of shorthand forms, hieroglyphs continued to be used well into the fourth century CE. For the Egyptians, hieroglyphs were both decorative and sacred, having been given to them by the god Thoth, according to their beliefs.

for many decades been a leading producer and distributor of music, film, and television throughout the Arab world, most Arabic speakers recognize and understand the Egyptian dialect.

The language of ancient Egypt, however, was Egyptian, an Afro-Asiatic language and one of the first-known written languages in the world. Egyptian hieroglyphic writing and Sumerian cuneiform seem to have developed around the same time, with the earliest Egyptian script appearing in the fourth millennium BCE. The spoken language evolved over the millennia, and scribes developed quick cursive forms of the glyphs for the sake of expediency. Even so, hieroglyphs were still used until Roman times.

Beginning in the seventh century, Arabic gradually replaced Egyptian after the Arabs conquered the country and the people began converting to Islam. The Egyptian language survived for many centuries within the Coptic community, although they began using Greek script to write it. They modified the alphabet by adding seven new characters (possibly derived from a simplified form of hieroglyphic script called demotic) to accommodate native Egyptian sounds. The Copts now speak Arabic, but they still use the old language in their religious rites.

Most educated Egyptians also speak English or French.

CHAPTER 6

CULTURE: COLLISION OF OLD AND NEW

Egypt's ancient monuments are some of the most impressive and widely renowned architectural achievements in the world. Thousands of years after the construction of the pyramids and the Sphinx, tourists are still flocking to Egypt to marvel at these ancient achievements.

The first pyramids were built at Saqqarah, just south of Memphis. The greatest was a step pyramid built for the pharaoh Djoser. The largest pyramid was built in approximately 2550 BCE for the pharaoh Khufu at Giza, just outside modern Cairo. It was made from 2.3 million blocks of stone. The blocks were fit together with precision to form a structure with four identical sloping sides that met perfectly at a center point 480 feet (146 m) high. To finish the structure, the blocks were covered with a bright white layer of smooth limestone. Remarkably, the pyramids were built during a period of less than 30 years and without the use of

The skyline of Cairo shows many characteristics of Egyptian architecture, including domes and minarets.

wheels or modern machinery—despite the fact that much of the stone was brought in from off-site quarries.

During the periods of Arab, Mamluk, and Ottoman rule, new Islamic architectural styles emerged. They were preserved in Old Cairo, which is today a treasure trove of medieval Islamic architecture, containing many mosques with domes and minarets, palaces, and *wakalat* (originally, inns for accommodating traveling traders). These mosques boast decorative stone facades, windows, arches, and courtyards, which served as marketplaces. One notable example, Wakalat El Ghoury, was built in 1505 and now serves as a cultural center and school of handicrafts.

In the nineteenth century, Isma'il Pasha sought to modernize and Westernize Egypt. Under his rule, many magnificent and ornate buildings in European styles sprung up in Cairo, built by French and Italian architects. Cairo came to be known as the "Paris of the Nile." Many of these buildings have since fallen into decay, as their current landlords have

PTOLEMY'S LIGHTHOUSE

In the third century BCE, Ptolemy II commissioned the building of an enormous 40-story lighthouse on the island of Pharos, off Alexandria. In its day, it immediately became a tourist attraction and was regarded as one of the Seven Wonders of the World. The lighthouse survived for approximately 1,500 years, withstanding earthquakes and tsunamis, but then finally crumbled around 1323 CE. However, its architectural legacy lives on, and even the name *Pharos* has become synonymous with lighthouses.

neither the money nor the incentive to finance their restoration and maintenance.

MUSIC AND DANCE

Classical Egyptian music is of Arab origin and therefore uses the main Arabic instruments: the oud (a lute), the qanun (a string instrument), the nai (a flute), the violin, the tabla (a hand drum), and the tambourine. Egypt also has regional folk music, such as the saïdi, which is characterized by a distinctive heavy beat and use of the rebab (a traditional violin) and the mizmar (a traditional wind instrument like the oboe that emits a high, sharp sound).

The sphinx has the face of a man and the body of a lion.

The most beloved figure in Egyptian music is undoubtedly Umm Kulthum. She was known for her rich voice, her improvisational skill, and her deep emotional connection with the audience. Just one song in her live performances could last for hours, depending on the audience's reaction. She began performing publicly in the 1920s, reached her peak in the 1940s and 1950s, and performed into the early 1970s. When she died in 1975, her funeral was attended by more than 4 million mourners.

Today, Egyptian music still employs traditional rhythms and vocal styles, but it also incorporates electronic instruments and elements of Western pop music. Egyptian music is popular throughout the Arab world. Some current stars that have gained international fame are Amr Diab, Hakim, Tamer Hosny, and Shereen.

Egypt is famous for its world-class belly dancers, and Cairo has long been the belly-dancing capital of the world. In Egypt, this art form is known as *raqs sharqi*, or "Eastern dance." Belly dancing is also popular throughout the Middle East and northern Africa, and each country has developed its own distinct style. Many famous Egyptian dancers—such as Nagwa Fouad, Naima Akef, Tahiyya Karioka, Samia Gamal, and Suheir Zaki—have appeared and danced in Egyptian movies.

TELEVISION AND FILM

Cairo was the original center of the Arab film industry, and Egypt is still

BELLY DANCING

Even though belly dancing continues to grow in popularity around the world, it seems to be declining in popularity in Egypt. The two primary reasons for its decline are the expense of going to a nightclub to see a professional show and the rise in religiosity and conservatism. Egyptian dancers today are concerned about losing their cultural heritage. Many are asking the government for support in preserving the art.

Professional belly dancers occupy a strange place in Egyptian society. Their skill is admired and celebrated, but they carry a stigma. Most Egyptian people do not consider belly dancing to be an art. Many ordinary Egyptians, male and female, learn to dance to traditional rhythms and enjoy this form of dancing at weddings and parties. But for a girl to become a professional belly dancer is considered a disgrace to her family.

Belly dancing is popular throughout the Middle East, but especially in Egypt.

Egyptian actor Omar Sharif, *left*, shares a scene with
Peter O'Toole in the 1962 movie *Lawrence of Arabia*.

a top producer of Arabic movies and television programs. Egyptians
started producing films in the 1920s, the first of which was a silent
movie, *In the Land of Tutankhamun*, in 1923. Since then, they have produced
countless films and spawned stars such as Hoda Sultan, Leila Mourad, and

Omar Sharif. Sharif has acted in European and American films and was nominated for an Oscar for his role in *Lawrence of Arabia* in 1962.

Television is the most popular entertainment medium in Egypt. Popular programs include entertainment shows for teens, talk shows for adults, children's programs, and musical performances and videos. Egyptian television stations also broadcast educational and religious programs and sports. Egyptian soap operas are popular across the Arab world, particularly during the month of Ramadan, when special holiday programs are released.

LITERATURE

The Egyptians were among the first to write narrative stories, but little remains of the culture's ancient literature. Among modern Egyptian writers, the most famous is Naguib Mahfouz. His novels, plays, and screenplays explore the many layers of Egyptian society, past and present, and are often dark and socially critical. He is credited for making the novel a popular art form in Arabic. His most famous works are the *Cairo Trilogy* and *The Harafish*.

'Ala' al-Aswani is one of the most popular novelists in Egypt today. His *Yacoubian Building* (2002) is a sharp criticism of the corruption and hypocrisy found today in Egyptian government and society.

CELEBRATIONS

Because Egypt is a predominantly Islamic country, many of its biggest celebrations are Islamic holidays. The biggest of these is Ramadan, which takes place during the ninth month of the Islamic calendar. During this month, fasting from sunrise to sundown is expected of everyone except the very old, the very young, the ill, and pregnant and breast-feeding women. The purpose of fasting is for people to understand their own weakness and dependence on God. However, at sundown families get together for the *iftar*, the breaking of the fast, which is usually a big meal consisting of special dishes served only during this month. After the big meal, Egyptian cities are abuzz with people eager to socialize. Schools and businesses run on a special schedule. Special Ramadan programs are run on television. Muslims go to mosques for special prayers at night, called *tarawih*.

The Eid el-Fitr marks the end of the month of Ramadan. This holiday lasts for three days and is traditionally celebrated by buying new clothes and giving children presents. Also at this time, Muslims are expected to give to charity.

The other big Islamic holiday is the Eid el-Adha, the tenth day of the twelfth month of the Islamic calendar. This three-day celebration commemorates the biblical story in which God asks Abraham to sacrifice his son Ishmael but then stops him at the last minute. This holiday is celebrated with the sacrifice of a lamb, which is then cooked and shared with family. Traditionally, part of the lamb should be shared with the poor.

A typical *iftar* during Ramadan includes foods such as dried fruits and nuts served with tea or coffee.

Moulids are a type of religious festival celebrated by both Muslims and Christians. *Moulid* means "birthday," and these celebrations are held in honor of saints, holy men, and founders of Sufi orders. Moulid al Nabi, for example, commemorates the Prophet Muhammad's birthday. Moulids are carnival-like, joyous celebrations, with parades, music, chanting, dancing, decorations, and other special events. However, these holidays are also a time for prayer and spiritual reflection. Conservative groups such as the Muslim Brotherhood condemn moulids as un-Islamic. Even so, they remain a popular expression of the traditionally relaxed, Sufi-based Islam traditionally practiced by most Egyptians.

WEDDINGS

Weddings in Egypt are big affairs. Traditionally, the bride and groom are married by a religious official, after which they are led to the wedding reception by a *zaffa*—a traditional, festive procession of musicians and belly dancers. The wedding guests follow, clapping and singing, and women trill their tongues loudly in celebration, making a special sound known as the *zaghruta*. Upon arriving at the location of the reception, the bride and groom, like a king and queen, are seated on a dais (a *kosha*), or a special seat in front of the room.

FOOD

Many foods that Egyptians enjoy are similar to foods from Middle Eastern countries: falafel, tahini, pita bread, shawarma (thinly sliced spiced meat), *kuftah* (spiced ground beef or lamb patties), *gibna* (a white cheese similar to feta), and stuffed vegetables. Common desserts include fruits, baklava, and rice pudding.

Some dishes that are unique to Egypt are *mulukhiyyah*, *koshary*, and *ful mudammis*. Mulukhiyyah is made from the edible green leaves of the jute plant, which are stewed with garlic and meat or chicken. Koshary is a mix of rice, pasta, and brown lentils served with tomato sauce, a spicy tangy garlic sauce, and fried onions. It is the most common type of fast food in Egypt and can be found almost everywhere. Ful mudammis is a simple dish made with fava beans, olive oil, onions, garlic, lemon juice, parsley, cumin, and sometimes tomatoes. It is commonly eaten for breakfast.

Pork products are not found in most Egyptian cuisine, because eating them is forbidden under Islam. However, some Coptic Christians raise pigs to be eaten within their community. Coptic Christians are also allowed to drink wine in moderation, while alcohol is taboo for Muslims. Most Egyptians prefer to drink soda, fresh fruit juices, *laban rayeb* (a yogurt drink, which may or may not be sweetened), *karkady* (hibiscus tea that is often served sweetened and iced), and Turkish-style coffee.

COFFEEHOUSES

A coffeehouse is the traditional gathering place for young and old (although usually just men). There, they meet friends and drink coffee or tea, smoke the *sheesha* (a water pipe filled with plain or honey-soaked flavored tobacco), play backgammon, and talk. Coffeehouses can be found on almost all the street corners in Egyptian cities.

MOHAMED ABOU-TRIKA

Mohamed Abou-Trika is considered one of the most talented soccer players in Egypt. In 2011, he was a midfielder on the successful Al Ahly soccer club. In the 2008 Africa Cup, Abou-Trika was penalized for displaying a pro-Palestinian slogan, "Sympathize with Gaza," in violation of a rule against displaying political views. At the time, Israel had imposed tight sanctions against the Palestinians of the Gaza Strip, and Abou-Trika was attempting to send a humanitarian message to people watching the game. His action drew an overwhelming outpouring of support for him, along with strong criticism for the referee who issued the penalty. These responses demonstrated Egyptians' strong feelings about the situation in Gaza, as well as their solidarity with the Palestinians.

SPORTS

Many sports are popular in Egypt, including handball, squash, swimming, and basketball, as well as snorkeling and diving in the Red Sea region. However, among all sports, soccer is definitely king.

Egypt has a strong national soccer league, and its games are broadcast around the Middle East. The national team won the Africa Cup of Nations in 2010, the third victory in a row (and seventh overall, out of 22 competitions total).[1] Among Egypt's recent star players are Mohamed Zidan, Ahmed Hassan, Wael Gomaa, Essam El Hadary, and Mohamed Abou-Trika.

Egyptian soccer player Mohamed Abou-Trika celebrates after scoring a goal in the 2008 Africa Cup.

CHAPTER 7

POLITICS: A COUNTRY IN TRANSITION

In the decades leading up to 2011, Egypt was a democracy in name only, as an authoritarian government suppressed all opposition. Officially, Egypt held elections for president and parliamentary seats. But in reality, the nation was only a "pantomime democracy."[1] During each election cycle, there was a big show of campaigning, but few outside the ruling party—the National Democratic Party (NDP)—ever had a real chance of getting elected. The NDP held the presidency and most of the seats in parliament.

In addition, corruption and nepotism abounded. Before 2011, it was clear that President Hosni Mubarak was grooming his son Gamal to succeed him in the presidency. Mubarak's regime was known for harassing and suppressing its opposition, intimidating voters, hampering freedom of speech, and even using torture.

Egyptians read newspapers showing the historical news of President Hosni Mubarak's resignation, in Tahrir Square, Cairo.

In the 2005 election, for example, Mubarak received 88.6 percent of the vote, despite being wildly unpopular with the Egyptian people. His opponents, Ayman Nour and Noman Gomaa, received 7.6 percent and 2.9 percent of the vote, respectively.[2] Analysts have estimated that only 18 percent of the population even voted in the election—a sign of widespread apathy and resignation.

In early 2011, the Egyptian people decided they wanted a real democracy. Frustrated after almost 60 years of one-party rule, police brutality, and limits on freedom of expression, thousands of Egyptians protested in Cairo and elsewhere. On February 11, after the military joined in support of the people, Mubarak gave in to the immense pressure to resign. But who would replace him remained undecided.

LOOKING TO THE FUTURE

Following Mubarak's resignation, the Supreme Council of the Armed Forces took charge of the government and disbanded the parliament. Essam Abdel Aziz Sharaf was appointed to serve as prime minister on March 4, 2011. A new cabinet was sworn in on March 7. The Supreme Council, prime minister, and cabinet comprised the interim government until new elections could be held. They planned to hold free elections for parliament in September 2011 and for president no later than November 2011. While some Egyptians supported the military's efforts to transition

The Egyptian flag features the national emblem: a golden eagle with a shield on its chest.

A woman holds a sign that reads, "I love you my country," as hundreds of Egyptian women line up at a polling place to vote on a constitutional referendum on March 19, 2011.

power swiftly, others argued that not enough time was being allowed for the long-oppressed people to form political parties and choose candidates. And while many hoped for democracy, some feared that rushing to form a new government would result in putting another authoritarian figure or a religious extremist in office.

On March 19, 2011, Egyptians approved several constitutional changes. Previously, only members of the National Democratic Party and other small, recognized parties could run for president. Independents could run only after being endorsed by 250 elected officials. Now candidates would need only one of the following: support of 30 members of parliament; signatures of 30,000 eligible voters; or a nomination by a recognized political party. Instead of unlimited six-year terms, presidents now would be limited to two four-year terms. To deter election tampering, elections would have full judicial oversight. The judicial branch was granted power to determine eligibility of elected officials. If a future president wanted

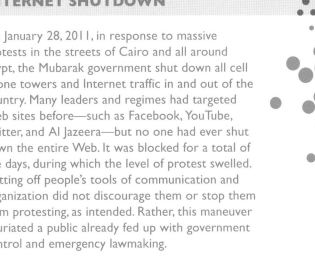

INTERNET SHUTDOWN

On January 28, 2011, in response to massive protests in the streets of Cairo and all around Egypt, the Mubarak government shut down all cell phone towers and Internet traffic in and out of the country. Many leaders and regimes had targeted Web sites before—such as Facebook, YouTube, Twitter, and Al Jazeera—but no one had ever shut down the entire Web. It was blocked for a total of five days, during which the level of protest swelled. Cutting off people's tools of communication and organization did not discourage them or stop them from protesting, as intended. Rather, this maneuver infuriated a public already fed up with government control and emergency lawmaking.

to declare a state of emergency, it would have to be approved by a majority in parliament and would be limited to a six-month period, unless Egyptians approve an extension by referendum. The country also planned to consider additional constitutional changes after a new government took power.

AUTHORITARIAN HISTORY

Egypt officially became a republic when Gamal Abdel Nasser came to power following the 1952 revolution and the exile of King Farouk. Nasser drafted a constitution in 1964, but a new one was issued in 1971 under the Anwar el-Sadat administration. It was amended under the same administration in 1980 and then again under Mubarak in 2005 and 2007. Many of the amendments made under Mubarak were aimed at reinforcing his power and extending his term in office.

ORGANIZATION OF
THE INTERIM GOVERNMENT OF EGYPT

Executive Branch	Judicial Branch
Supreme Council of the Armed Forces Prime Minister Cabinet	Supreme Constitutional Court

The original constitution guaranteed citizens many freedoms, such as freedom of speech and freedom from unlawful detainment. However, citizens' freedoms changed under the so-called emergency law—a constitutional provision put into effect after the assassination of Sadat and renewed indefinitely by the Mubarak regime. This law gave the government and police more power to censor the press, to detain people without due process, and to break up public protests. Mubarak's regime argued that the law was a necessary tool in the fight against terrorism, but in reality, it was used more frequently to limit free speech and political activism. After Mubarak's fall, the military promised to suspend this practice.

Under the same constitution, the Egyptian president had a cabinet of 37 ministers, which were presided over by the prime minister. All of these officials were appointed by the president. Mubarak's prime minister was Ahmad Nazif. His cabinet also included ambassadors, the nation's official representative to the United Nations, and the governor of the Central Bank.

Egypt's bicameral parliament, which was disbanded by the military government in February 2011, consisted of an Advisory Council (Shura Council) with 264 seats (176 elected by popular vote, 88 appointed) and a People's Assembly with 518 seats (508 elected by popular vote, 10 appointed). In the People's Assembly, 64 seats were reserved for women. Members of the Advisory Council, who served mostly as consultants, had six-year terms. Members of the People's Assembly, the more influential of the two houses in forming legislation, had five-year terms.

Egypt's legal system has been based on both Islamic and civil law. In particular, it was influenced by the Napoleonic Code, the French civil code established in 1804 under Napoléon I, which held that all citizens were equal before the law. The Napoleonic Code served as the prototype for the legal systems of many European and colonial countries in the nineteenth century. Egypt's Supreme Constitutional Court interprets laws and the constitution, enforces laws, and settles disputes from lower courts.

OPPOSITION

While disagreement was discouraged under the Mubarak government, several opposition groups grew powerful. The Muslim Brotherhood has become the largest and most organized of these groups. Its goals are to

THE MUSLIM BROTHERHOOD

Founded in the 1920s, the Muslim Brotherhood gained popular support through its charity work. Under Mubarak, the group still focused on helping the poor in areas where the government was failing to do so. In addition, the brotherhood provided an organized alternative to the Mubarak regime, with which so many Egyptians were frustrated.

Following the 1952 Revolution, the brotherhood was brutally oppressed by the Nasser regime, and the Mubarak regime also restricted its operation. Not only did this treatment fail to damage the brotherhood's cause, but it also succeeded in making martyrs of the Brothers and in increasing the group's prestige among followers.

Muslim Brotherhood leader Mohammed Badie arrives for a press conference about fraud in parliamentary elections in November 2010.

Egyptian Nobel Peace laureate and democracy advocate Mohamed ElBaradei addresses a crowd of protestors who wanted to end the Mubarak regime at Tahrir Square in Cairo on January 30, 2011.

restore Egypt to a pure Islamic lifestyle and to establish a government based on sharia (Islamic) law. Because religious parties were banned from nominating candidates for election before 2011, the Muslim Brotherhood was unable to participate in the nation's decision making. Members of the organization won seats in the parliament as independents, although many of them were lost back to the ruling party in 2010.

Another opposition group is the 6th of April Youth Movement, comprised of young, educated Egyptians. This organization started as a Facebook group in 2008, when it supported a labor strike. In early 2011, the group was one of the main forces behind protests against the Mubarak regime.

The National Association for Change is an opposition group formed in 2010 by Egyptian national and Nobel Peace Prize laureate Mohamed ElBaradei. Several leaders of opposition political parties have joined the group, including Ayman Nour of the Tomorrow Party, who challenged Mubarak for the presidency in 2005; novelist 'Ala' al-Aswani; and even members of the Muslim Brotherhood.

MOHAMED ELBARADEI

Mohamed ElBaradei, born in Cairo in 1946, is the former director general of the International Atomic Energy Agency (IAEA), part of the United Nations. In 2005, he was awarded the Nobel Peace Prize, jointly with the IAEA, for efforts "to prevent nuclear energy from being used for military purposes and to ensure that nuclear energy for peaceful purposes is used in the safest possible way."[3] Although ElBaradei lived abroad for 30 years, his achievements and his strong campaigns for democratic change in his home country have made him popular among reform-minded Egyptians. In 2011, there was an active push to make him a presidential candidate.

CHAPTER 8

ECONOMICS: LIMITED OPPORTUNITIES

Between 1952 and 1970, President Gamal Abdel Nasser centralized Egypt's economy, nationalizing many large companies and establishing some socialist policies. However, in the 1970s, Anwar el-Sadat opened up the economy to foreign business, investment, and trade and to private-sector development. Mubarak continued to work toward privatization and encouraged foreign investment.

Despite these efforts at economic growth, Egypt is one of the poorest countries in the Middle East. Although it does have petroleum reserves in the Sinai Peninsula, the level of those reserves is nothing compared to the vast supplies of neighboring Saudi Arabia and the United Arab Emirates.

Due to the prevalence of poverty in Egypt, many Egyptians live in shacks such as these in Cairo.

CURRENCY

Egypt's currency is the Egyptian pound, which was valued at 5.92 to the US dollar in March 2011.[5] Egyptian coins are called piastres. One Egyptian pound is worth 100 piastres.

In 2010, Egypt's annual gross domestic product (GDP) was estimated at $500.9 billion, putting it at twenty-seventh among world economies.[1] However, the nation ranked 136th with regard to per capita GDP, or income per person, which was estimated at $6,200 the same year.[2] In 2008, the GDP growth rate of the country was approximately 7 percent.[3]

The global financial crisis that began in 2007 slowed economic growth in Egypt but did not hit the country as hard as expected. Egypt was spared in part because it was not heavily integrated with world financial markets. Stimulus programs at home, which invested in infrastructure and public projects, also helped cushion the blow, as did lowering interest rates. By 2010, economic growth was back to approximately 5.3 percent.[4]

Regardless, GDP growth has failed to keep up with Egypt's growing population, and it has failed to trickle down to the Egyptian people. The overall economy has remained weak, and the financial situation of the average Egyptian is the worst that it has been in 20 years. Approximately 44 percent of the population is considered poor or extremely poor. The average wage in Egypt is less than $100 per month, and unemployment

Egyptian pounds

is high.[6] A 2010 estimate put unemployment at 9.7 percent, but it may actually be much higher.[7] Studies of unemployment among youth estimate that 25 percent of young men and 59 percent of young women under age 25 are unemployed.[8]

With unemployment high and no unemployment insurance or other economic support, Egypt's middle class has been deteriorating, and the divide between rich and poor has grown. Many people have been forced to live in shantytowns and tents, children have been sent to work, and some public employees have taken bribes and kickbacks to supplement their income.

EGYPTIAN COTTON

Cotton has been a major cash crop in Egypt since the nineteenth century, when Muhammad 'Ali—then ruler of Egypt—initiated widespread planting and transformed the plant into a major export. Today, Egypt is the world's main producer of long-staple cotton. Sheets bearing the label "Egyptian cotton" have long been popular among people worldwide. The long, thin fibers of this cotton weave sturdy yet soft fabrics. Interestingly, the cloth preferred by the ancient Egyptians was linen, which was derived from the flax plant.

CHALLENGES

Government corruption and neglect of the lower class are widely seen as contributing to Egypt's economic problems. Many government ministers have personal interests in the businesses they are supposed to regulate. Politicians use their positions to engage in underhanded deals that benefit them but are not

Agriculture continues to be an important sector of
the Egyptian economy.

CAIRO'S RECYCLERS

The Zabbaleen are a group of mostly Coptic Christians that live in a neighborhood on the east side of Cairo, near the Muqatam hills. They have served as the city's unofficial trash collectors for a century. In years past, they collected garbage using donkey carts, and later, they began using trucks. After hauling the garbage home, they sort it. Today, plastic, scrap metal, and cardboard are among the items they recycle or resell.

Until 2009, the Zabbaleen also collected organic waste, such as discarded food from restaurants, schools, and grocery stores. They fed this waste to the pigs they raised as a source of food and income. However, in the summer of that year, the swine flu scare swept the globe, and people became worried about the safety of pork products from pigs that had eaten spoiled food. The Egyptian government responded by slaughtering approximately 400,000 pigs. This action eliminated a major source of income for the Zabbaleen and created a huge organic waste problem in Cairo.

in the public interest. Government officials receive priority housing in Cairo, while many poor Egyptians live in dangerous shantytowns, awaiting promised government housing aid that does not arrive. Fancy resorts, huge shopping malls, and sprawling suburbs cater to the privileged class and to tourists, while the majority of the population struggles to get by.

The Egyptian government spends approximately $2.74 billion a year to help offset the cost of staples such as bread, petroleum, sugar, tea, and cooking oil.[9] The government's efforts to absorb some of the cost keeps prices low for citizens, despite hikes in food prices worldwide. Unfortunately, this system—like many others in Egypt—is plagued by abuse and corruption. But given the savings it provides, combined with the fact that it has been in place since World War II, reforming or dismantling it would be nearly impossible. When Sadat tried to do so in 1977, bread riots broke out.

Corruption is a regular part of life in Egypt and occurs at all levels of society. For many people, being corrupt is the only way to get by. Property owners solicit bribes from tenants, inspectors get kickbacks from property owners, shop owners illegally resell government-subsidized items, and ordinary people buy and resell subsidized products at higher prices.

Furthermore, each year, Egypt receives hundreds of millions of dollars in economic aid from the United States ($250 million in 2010).[10] Ordinary Egyptians do not enjoy any benefits from this support, however. Part of the problem is that the population is large and growing at a rate of 2 percent per year.[11] This means that each person is entitled to only a couple of dollars in aid. Also, studies have not demonstrated any significant job growth or improvement in the financial market as a result of receiving the economic aid. According to the Carnegie Endowment for International Peace, Egypt needs to change tactics to use the aid more wisely. Changes might include creating more permanent job opportunities by investing in small businesses, funding programs that reclaim arable land for agriculture, and providing direct aid to the very poorest people.

Ancient Egyptian workers organized the first-known labor strike circa 1152 BCE.

In addition, Egypt received $1.3 billion per year in military aid from the United States when Mubarak was in power.[12] Egypt has been a key US ally in the Middle East, and maintaining its long-standing peace with Israel was vital to US foreign policy. Providing this form of aid ensured that Egypt's military would remain strong and that the nation would continue to respect the peace agreement with its neighbor, despite widespread feelings of resentment toward Israel and support for the Palestinian cause among the Egyptian people. This aid also helped Egypt purchase American-made weapons, which meant some of the money returned to the US economy. Finally, the investment in Egypt's military gave the United States priority access to Egyptian airspace and to the Suez Canal, which was important to US military involvement in the Middle East.

Cairo has Africa's only subway system.

INDUSTRIES, RESOURCES, AND TRADE

Throughout history, the Egyptian economy has been based on a strong agricultural sector. This is still true, although the service industry has surpassed agriculture as Egyptians' chief area of employment. The nation's main agricultural products are cotton, rice, corn, wheat, beans, fruits, and vegetables. Livestock include cattle, goats, water buffalo, and sheep.

The Egyptian government has been subsidizing staples such as bread.

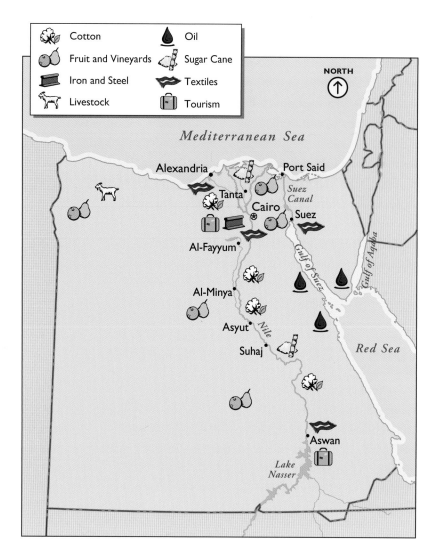

Resources of Egypt

Egypt's main industries are textiles, food processing, tourism, chemicals, pharmaceuticals, hydrocarbons, construction, cement, metals, and light manufacturing. Egypt is not terribly rich with natural resources, but it does have limited reserves of petroleum, natural gas, iron ore, manganese, phosphates, and limestone.

Egypt's main trading partners are the United States, China, Italy, Germany, Spain, India, Saudi Arabia, Syria, Turkey, France, and South Korea. In 2010, Egypt exported $25.34 billion in commodities and imported $46.52 billion worth.[13] Exports include crude oil and petroleum products, cotton, textiles, metal products, chemicals, and processed food. Imports include machinery and equipment, foodstuffs, chemicals, wood products, and fuels.

INFRASTRUCTURE

In the past 50 years, Egypt has made a great deal of progress in transportation, telecommunication, power, and sanitation. During the recent financial crisis, infrastructure investment stimulated growth. World Bank policy researchers have determined that Egypt would experience a direct GDP per capita increase if it increased spending on improving infrastructure in the future.

CHAPTER 9
EGYPT TODAY

For most of the year, the daily life of an Egyptian teenager involves primarily school and homework. For students in secondary school, preparing for the difficult final exam, the Thanawiyya Amma, dominates their thoughts. After school, many students spend extra time studying with private tutors.

When students are not studying, they are often spending time with their families at home. Egypt is a very family-oriented society, and young people have a strong bond and a strong sense of duty to their families. Families often include extended family members—grandparents, aunts, uncles, and cousins—who may live in the same house, building, or neighborhood, especially in rural areas. Egyptians usually live at home until they are married, so a high school graduate is not likely to strike out on his or her own at age 18. Some college students live in gender-segregated dormitories on campus, however.

A young girl has her face painted with the Egyptian flag at a unity rally in Tahrir Square on March 11, 2011.

Most middle-class teenagers do not have part-time jobs, but they may be responsible for performing household duties, caring for younger siblings, or helping with a family business. In poor communities and rural areas, however, it is much more common for teenagers and even young children to work to help support their struggling families—often leaving school to do so. The work they do is usually manual labor: cleaning and domestic work, factory and workshop labor, street vending, and traditional work in agriculture or handicrafts. Unfortunately, the need for children to help support their families seems to be increasing, with rising prices and approximately 20 percent of the country's population living under the official poverty line.[1]

For Egyptians, the weekend begins on Thursday night and goes through Saturday. The Islamic holy day is Friday. Religious teenagers attend mosques on Friday, but then they spend the rest of the weekend with their families and friends.

Egyptians were the first to use the 365-day calendar and to divide days into 24 hours.

In urban areas, well-off teenagers enjoy going to movies and watching television at home. Egypt produces a large volume of television programming, including comedies, soap operas, and religious programs. Sports—especially soccer matches—are popular as well. Young people also enjoy visiting shopping malls and Internet cafés, playing sports in sporting clubs, and walking along the water (in Cairo, the Nile; in Alexandria, the Mediterranean). Options for entertainment are more limited in rural areas, so young people often get together and play soccer.

Young Egyptian women dress conservatively in hijabs but show their personal style with bright colors and designs.

CONSERVATIVE PRACTICES

Egypt is a fairly conservative society, and Muslims and Christians alike follow social norms that may seem restrictive to Western teens. For example, while young men and women attend school together, their socializing after school in private settings is generally not considered appropriate. Young men and women can be together in public places and at publicly organized parties, concerts, and get-togethers, but a young woman would never meet a young man at his house or be alone with him in a private setting.

Dating is less common in Egypt than in the West, and many marriages are arranged. Couples sometimes go out and perhaps sit close together or walk hand in hand, but more intimate public displays of affection are

THE HIJAB

Over the past few decades, Egypt has become more outwardly conservative. In the 1950s and 1960s, most middle- and upper-class women did not wear the hijab, which they associated with the lower class. But today, few women or teenage girls would be seen without it. Some choose to wear the hijab as a reaction against Western cultural domination and in assertion of their Muslim identity and pride. Others wear it to follow the social trend.

Wearing a hijab also sends a message to men about a young woman's character. If she is wearing the head scarf, then she is seen as a good Muslim and commands respect. This recognition has become increasingly important as more and more women have left home to go to school or to enter the workforce, where they interact with men. Wearing the hijab gives women more freedom to associate with men without worrying about harassment.

A young girl sits outside her family's house
in El-Kharga doing schoolwork.

not acceptable. Dating practices in rural areas tend to be even more conservative.

Most young women dress modestly in clothes that are loose fitting and cover the arms and legs. The majority wear the hijab, or Muslim head scarf. Yet many young women also care about fashion. They enjoy tying their hijabs in different styles and matching their hijabs to their outfits. They also prefer to wear clothes with colors and designs, rather than the plain, black attire worn by women in stricter Arab countries, such as Saudi Arabia.

Some young women push the limits of modesty by wearing tighter-fitting, stylish clothes and lots of makeup. But most would not be bold enough to wear the tightly fitted, skin-baring outfits commonly worn by Egyptian pop singers such as Ruby in the video clips that are so popular among young people in Egypt.

Young men have more leeway in what they wear, because their reputation and behavior are not as closely protected as those of young women. Even so, most young men care about their appearance and wear nice shirts and long pants when they go out. Jeans and soccer jerseys are also common, but shorts are never worn.

Egyptians eat three meals a day, with the main meal being served at lunch.

EDUCATION

Egypt has a free, government-run system of universal public education, which includes primary, preparatory, secondary, and university levels. Primary and preparatory school attendance for both males and females (ages 6 to 15) is required, but many poor families take their children out of school early to work.

School enrollment has increased over the past several decades, as more girls have been brought into the system. The literacy rate has increased, as well. In 2008, literacy was estimated at 72.4 percent.[2] But there is still progress to be made. The educational system is underfunded, with only 3.8 percent of the GDP spent in this area, and it is difficult for the system to keep up with Egypt's rapidly growing population.[3]

From the 1960s to the 1980s, college graduates were guaranteed a government job under a policy enacted by Nasser to encourage education. However, as the number of graduates grew, this system became less and less practical, and it was abolished in 1989. Today, thousands of frustrated students graduate from college every year, only to find that jobs are hard to come by or that they lack the skills required to get specific jobs in the private sector. Some parents and students feel this situation could be helped by reforming the school system so it would better prepare students for diverse careers.

CHALLENGES AND FUTURE OUTLOOK

Egypt faces many challenges. Economically, its middle class is strained, as people face poverty, inflation, rising food prices, and unemployment. The education system is in need of reform, and child labor and lack of health care have taken their toll on the population. Politically, the country entered a state of transition in 2011 that the Egyptian people hoped would result in free elections and formation of a democratic government. Socially, there has been tension between Muslims and Copts and between radical Muslims and moderate Muslims, and secular Egyptians have been sidelined.

"The international community must understand we are being denied every human right day by day. Egypt today is one big prison. If the international community does not speak out it will have a lot of implications. We are fighting for universal values here. If the West is not going to speak out now, then when?"[4]

—*Mohamed ElBaradei, Egyptian lawyer and government official*

With the establishment of a true democracy, in which all citizens can participate, these issues may be addressed. Egypt has gone through many periods of decline and renewal during its long history. Now may be the time for the old dynasty to end and a new golden age to begin.

An Egyptian woman prays for her country's future
while reading from the Koran in February 2011.

TIMELINE

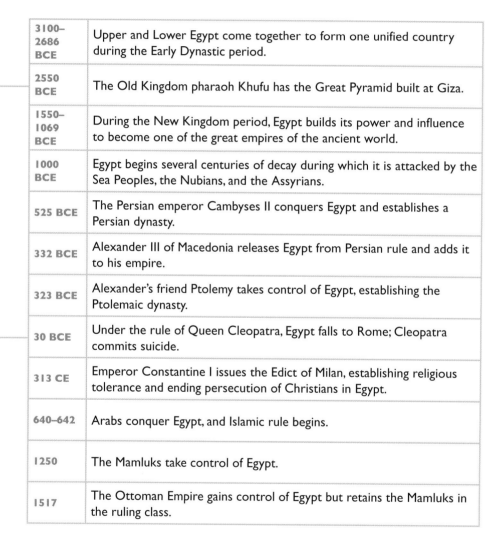

3100–2686 BCE	Upper and Lower Egypt come together to form one unified country during the Early Dynastic period.
2550 BCE	The Old Kingdom pharaoh Khufu has the Great Pyramid built at Giza.
1550–1069 BCE	During the New Kingdom period, Egypt builds its power and influence to become one of the great empires of the ancient world.
1000 BCE	Egypt begins several centuries of decay during which it is attacked by the Sea Peoples, the Nubians, and the Assyrians.
525 BCE	The Persian emperor Cambyses II conquers Egypt and establishes a Persian dynasty.
332 BCE	Alexander III of Macedonia releases Egypt from Persian rule and adds it to his empire.
323 BCE	Alexander's friend Ptolemy takes control of Egypt, establishing the Ptolemaic dynasty.
30 BCE	Under the rule of Queen Cleopatra, Egypt falls to Rome; Cleopatra commits suicide.
313 CE	Emperor Constantine I issues the Edict of Milan, establishing religious tolerance and ending persecution of Christians in Egypt.
640–642	Arabs conquer Egypt, and Islamic rule begins.
1250	The Mamluks take control of Egypt.
1517	The Ottoman Empire gains control of Egypt but retains the Mamluks in the ruling class.

1799	The Rosetta Stone is discovered by a French soldier.
1805	Muhammad 'Ali comes to power, establishing a modern Egyptian state. His successors rule Egypt until the 1952 Revolution.
1869	The Suez Canal opens, providing the fastest shipping route between Europe and the Indian Ocean.
1882	British forces occupy Egypt following a nationalist uprising against European intervention.
1919	Egyptians revolt against colonial rule.
1923	A constitutional monarchy is declared.
1936	King Farouk I ascends the throne.
1948	Egypt is defeated in the Palestine War.
1952	On July 23, the Free Officers, led by Gamal Abdel Nasser, depose King Farouk I and establish military rule.
1971	On September 11, a new constitution is put in place.
1981	In October 6, Anwar el-Sadat is assassinated by extremists; his vice president, Hosni Mubarak, succeeds him.
2011	On January 25, massive peaceful protests begin in opposition to the Mubarak regime. On February 11, Mubarak resigns.

[FACTS AT YOUR FINGERTIPS]

GEOGRAPHY

Official name: Arab Republic of Egypt (in Arabic, Jumhuriyat Misr al-Arabiyah)

Area: 386,662 square miles (1,001,450 sq km)

Climate: Desert

Highest elevation: Mount Katrina, 8,625 feet (2,629 m) above sea level

Lowest elevation: Qattara Depression, 436 feet (133 m) below sea level

Significant geographic features: Western Desert, Eastern Desert, Nile River

PEOPLE

Population (July 2011 est.): 82,079,636

Most populous city: Cairo

Ethnic groups: Ethnic Egyptian, Bedouin, Nubian, Berber

Percent of residents living in urban areas: 43 percent

Life expectancy: 72.66 years

Language: Arabic

Religions: Sunni Muslim, 90 percent; Coptic Christian, 9 percent; other Christian, 1 percent

GOVERNMENT AND ECONOMY

Government: Republic

Capital: Cairo

Date of adoption of current constitution: September 11, 1971 (amended March 19, 2011)

Head of state: President

Head of government: Prime minister

Legislature: Parliament, consists of the Advisory Council and the People's Assembly

Currency: Egyptian pound

Industries and natural resources: Textiles, food processing, tourism, construction, petroleum, cotton, textiles, metal products, chemicals

NATIONAL SYMBOLS

Holidays: Ramadan is an Islamic holiday taking place during the ninth month of the Islamic calendar. Coptic Christians celebrate Easter in April. Wafaa' al-Nil is a festival in August marking the annual flooding of the Nile.

Flag: Three horizontal bands of red, white, and black, bearing the national emblem (the Eagle of Saladin, a golden eagle with a shield on its chest)

National anthem: "Bilady, Bilady, Bilady" (My Homeland, My Homeland, My Homeland)

National symbol: The Eagle of Saladin, a golden eagle with a shield on its chest

KEY PEOPLE

Tutankhamen, boy pharaoh who became famous after his tomb was discovered in 1922

Cleopatra, queen of Egypt during the first century BCE

Gamal Abdel Nasser, president from 1956 to 1970 who established Islamic socialism

Hosni Mubarak, president from 1981 until he resigned amidst protests in 2011

Naguib Mahfouz, Nobel Prize–winning author

GOVERNORATE; CAPITAL

Al-Bahr al-Ahmar; Al-Ghardaqah

Al-Buhayrah; Damanhur

Al-Daqahliyyah; Al-Mansurah

Al-Fayyum; Aa-Fayyum

Al-Gharbiyah; Tanta

Al-Iskandariyah; Alexandria

Al-Isma'iliyyah; Ismailia

Al-Jizah; Al-Jizah

Al-Minufiyah; Shibin Al-Kawm

Al-Minya; Al-Minya

Al-Qalyubiyah; Banha

Al-Wadi al-Jadid; Al-Kharijah

Ash-Sharqiyah; Az-Zaqaziq

Aswan; Aswan

Asyut; Asyut

Bani Suwayf; Bani Suwayf

Cairo; Cairo

Dumyat; Damietta

Janub Sina; At-Tur

Kafr al-Shaykh; Kafr al-Shaykh

Luxor; Luxor

Matruh; Marsa Matruh

Port Said; Port Said

Qina; Qina

Shamal Sina; Al-Arish

Suez; Suez

Suhaj; Suhaj

GLOSSARY

adhan

The Islamic call to prayer, broadcast from the minaret of a mosque.

arable

Fertile and fit for agriculture.

Bedouins

A tribal, nomadic desert people of the Arabian Peninsula and northern Africa.

caliph

Civil and religious leader of the Muslim community.

Copts

Egyptian Christians who have their own denomination and follow their own pope, Pope Shenoudah III.

demotic

An extremely simplified version of hieroglyphic writing, created by scribes for efficiency.

hieratic

A simplified version of hieroglyphic writing used in sacred texts.

hijab

A Muslim head scarf.

hyrax

A small, furry herbivorous mammal that resembles a guinea pig but whose closest relative is actually the elephant.

ibex

A type of wild goat with long, curved horns that generally inhabits rocky, mountainous terrain.

khamsin

A powerful desert windstorm.

koshary

A popular Egyptian street food/fast food consisting of lentils, rice, pasta, and fried onions and served with tomato sauce and hot sauce.

muezzin

The Muslim who issues the daily call to prayer.

nepotism

Favoritism shown toward family members in business or political situations.

oasis

A fertile area in a desert, centered around a spring or other water source.

pharaonic

Relating to ancient Egypt in the time of the pharaohs.

souk

An Arab marketplace or bazaar.

wadi

A valley or streambed that is wet during the rainy season but otherwise dry.

ADDITIONAL RESOURCES

SELECTED BIBLIOGRAPHY

Bradley, John R. *Inside Egypt: The Land of the Pharaohs on the Brink of a Revolution.* New York: Palgrave Macmillan, 2008. Print.

Rodenbeck, Max. *Cairo: The City Victorious.* New York: Knopf, 1998. Print.

Thompson, Jason. *A History of Egypt: From Earliest Times to the Present.* New York: Vintage Books, 2008. Print.

FURTHER READINGS

Al-Aswani, 'Ala'. *Friendly Fire: Stories.* New York: HarperCollins, 2009. Print.

Amin, Galal. *Whatever Else Happened to the Egyptians? From the Revolution to the Age of Globalization.* New York: American University in Cairo Press, 2004. Print.

Goldschmidt, Arthur, Jr. *A Brief History of Egypt.* New York: Facts on File, 2008. Print.

Gray, Leon. *The New Cultural Atlas of Egypt.* New York: Marshall Cavendish, 2010. Print.

WEB LINKS

To learn more about Egypt, visit ABDO Publishing Company online at **www.abdopublishing.com**. Web sites about Egypt are featured on our Book Links page. These links are routinely monitored and updated to provide the most current information available.

PLACES TO VISIT

If you are ever in Egypt, consider visiting these important and interesting sites!

Khan al-Khalili Bazaar

This huge market in the heart of Cairo is a popular shopping destination for Egyptians and tourists.

The Museum of Egyptian Antiquities, Cairo

Open since 1902, the museum's collection includes items from King Tutankhamen's tomb, mummies, and other treasures of ancient Egypt.

Pyramids of Giza

Located outside Cairo, these pyramids were constructed as burial tombs for the pharaohs of Memphis. The largest—the Great Pyramid built for Egyptian pharaoh Khufu—is more than 4,500 years old.

SOURCE NOTES

CHAPTER 1. A VISIT TO EGYPT

1. Ibn Battuta. Travels in Asia and Africa 1325–1354. London: Broadway House, 1929. Print. 50.

2. Tom Phillips. "Egyptian Cleric: Call to Prayer Ringtones Are 'Confusing.'" *Metro.* Associated Newspapers Limited, 22 Jan. 2010. Web. 2 Mar. 2011.

3. Emily Parker. "Alaa Al Aswany: The Writer Speaks Out on What Plagues Egypt." *The Wall Street Journal.* Dow Jones & Company, 29 Oct. 2008. Web. 2 Mar. 2011.

CHAPTER 2. GEOGRAPHY: LAND OF THE NILE

1. "Egypt's Administrative Division." *Egypt State Information Service.* Egypt State Information Service, 2006. Web. 2 Mar. 2011.

2. "The World Factbook: Egypt." *Central Intelligence Agency.* Central Intelligence Agency, 14 Feb. 2011. Web. 2 Mar. 2011.

3. "Basic Information." *Embassy of Egypt.* Egyptian Embassy, Washington DC, n.d. Web. 2 Mar. 2011.

4. "The World Factbook: Egypt." *Central Intelligence Agency.* Central Intelligence Agency, 14 Feb. 2011. Web. 2 Mar. 2011.

5. Justin Pollard and Howard Reid. *The Rise and Fall of Alexandria: Birthplace of the Modern Mind.* New York: Penguin, 2006. Print. 281.

6. "Land and People." *Egypt State Information Service.* Egypt State Information Service, 2006. Web. 12 Mar. 2011.

7. "Country Guide: Egypt." BBC: *Weather.* BBC, n.d. Web. 2 Mar. 2011.

CHAPTER 3. ANIMALS AND NATURE: ANCIENT SYMBOLS

1. "Summary Statistics: Summaries by Country, Table 5, Threatened Species in Each Country." *IUCN Red List of Threatened Species*. International Union for Conservation of Nature and Natural Resources, 2010. Web. 18 Jan. 2011.

2. "Protectorates: Natural Protectorates and Biodiversity." *Ministry of State for Environmental Affairs*. Egyptian Environmental Affairs Agency, 2010. Web. 2 Mar. 2011.

3. "The World Factbook: Egypt." *Central Intelligence Agency*. Central Intelligence Agency, 14 Feb. 2011. Web. 2 Mar. 2011.

CHAPTER 4. HISTORY: WHERE CIVILIZATION BEGAN

None.

CHAPTER 5. PEOPLE: MODERN EGYPTIANS

1. "The World Factbook: Egypt." *Central Intelligence Agency*. *Central Intelligence Agency*, 14 Feb. 2011. Web. 2 Mar. 2011.

2. Mona Khalifa, Julie DaVanzo, and David M. Adamson. "Population Growth in Egypt: A Continuing Policy Challenge." *Rand Corporation*. Rand Corporation, 2000. Web. 2 Mar. 2011.

3. "The World Factbook: Egypt." *Central Intelligence Agency*. Central Intelligence Agency, 14 Feb. 2011. Web. 2 Mar. 2011.

4. Ibid.

5. "The World Factbook: Egypt." *Central Intelligence Agency*. Central Intelligence Agency, 14 Feb. 2011. Web. 2 Mar. 2011.

6. "Former UN Secretary—General Boutros Boutros-Ghali: 'The Massacre in Alexandria Will Strengthen Our Bonds.'" *Spiegel Online International*. Spiegel, 12 Jan. 2011. Web. 2 Mar. 2011.

SOURCE NOTES CONTINUED

CHAPTER 6. CULTURE: COLLISION OF OLD AND NEW

1. "Africa Cup of Nations: Presentation and Medal Winners." *The-Sports.org*. Info Média Conseil, n.d. Web. 28 Feb. 2011.

CHAPTER 7. POLITICS: A COUNTRY IN TRANSITION

1. Abigail Hauslohner. "Egypt's Elections and Pantomime Democracy." *Time.com*. Time, 27 Nov. 2010. Web. 2 Mar. 2011.

2. "The World Factbook: Egypt." *Central Intelligence Agency*. Central Intelligence Agency, 14 Feb. 2011. Web. 2 Mar. 2011.

3. "Mohamed ElBaradei: Biography." *Nobelprize.org*. The Official Website of the Nobel Prize, 2005. Web. 2 Mar. 2011.

CHAPTER 8. ECONOMICS: LIMITED OPPORTUNITIES

1. "The World Factbook: Egypt." *Central Intelligence Agency*. Central Intelligence Agency, 14 Feb. 2011. Web. 2 Mar. 2011.

2. Ibid.

3. Ibid.

4. Ibid.

5. "Currency Converter." *Bloomberg*. Bloomberg, n.d. Web. 22 Feb. 2011.

6. "Will the Dam Burst?" *The Economist*. The Economist, 11 Sept. 2008. Web. 2 Mar. 2011.

7. "The World Factbook: Egypt." *Central Intelligence Agency*. Central Intelligence Agency, 14 Feb. 2011. Web. 2 Mar. 2011.

8. Mounira Chaieb. "Young in the Arab World: Egypt." *BBC News*. BBC New, 16 Feb. 2005. Web. 2 Mar. 2011.

9. "Land and People." *Egypt State Information Service*. Egypt State Information Service, 2006. Web. 12 Mar. 2011.

10. Susan Cornwell and Jim Wolf. "Factbox: Most U.S. Aid Goes to Military." *Reuters*. Reuters, 29 Jan. 2011. Web. 2 Mar. 2011.

11. Will Rasmussen. "Egypt fights to stem rapid population growth." *The New York Times*. The New York Times Company, 2 July 2008. Web. 17 Mar. 2011.

12. "Background Note: Egypt." *US Department of State*. US Department of State, 10 Nov. 2010. Web. 9 Mar. 2011.

13. "The World Factbook: Egypt." *Central Intelligence Agency*. Central Intelligence Agency, 14 Feb. 2011. Web. 2 Mar. 2011.

CHAPTER 9. EGYPT TODAY

1. "The World Factbook: Egypt." *Central Intelligence Agency*. Central Intelligence Agency, 14 Feb. 2011. Web. 2 Mar. 2011.

2. "UIS Statistics in Brief." *UNESCO Institute for Statistics*. UNESCO Institute for Statistics, n.d. Web. 15 Jan. 2011.

3. "The World Factbook: Egypt." *Central Intelligence Agency*. Central Intelligence Agency, 14 Feb. 2011. Web. 2 Mar. 2011.

4. Jack Shenker and Haroon Siddique. "Egyptian Government on Last Legs, Says ElBaradei." *Guardian.co.uk*. The Guardian, 28 Jan. 2011. Web. 2 Mar. 2011.

INDEX

PHOTO CREDITS

iStockphoto, cover, 2, 35, 52, 128 (bottom); Mohamed El-Dakhakhny/AP Images, 5 (top), 49;
Joel Carillet/iStockphoto, 5 (middle), 14, 121; Viktor Chornobay/iStockphoto, 5 (bottom), 75;
Miroslav Beneda/Fotolia, 6; ALFRED/SIPA/AP Images, 9, 94, 129; Matt Kania/Map Hero, Inc., 11,
22, 26, 71, 116; Ben Curtis/AP Images, 16; Fotolia, 18; Oleg Znamenskiy/Shutterstock Images, 24;
Anthon Jackson/Shutterstock Images, 29; Sergey Ponomarev/AP Images, 30; Natalia Lukiyanova/
iStockphoto, 33; Lucian Coman/Shutterstock Images, 36; Shutterstock Images, 39, 109, 133; Luke
Daniek/iStockphoto, 44, 128 (top); Steven Senne/AP Images, 56; Georgios Kollidas/iStockphoto,
59; AP Images, 64; Bill Foley/AP Images, 67; Peter Prengaman/AP Images, 68; Tara Todras-
Whitehill/AP Images, 73, 127; Bernice Williams/Shutterstock Images, 77, 130; Mikael Damkier/
Shutterstock Images, 80, 131; Michael Hind/Shutterstock Images, 84; Columbia Pictures/
Photofest, 86; Amelia Johnson/iStockphoto, 89; Rebecca Blackwell/AP Images, 93; Vladimir
Wrangel/Shutterstock Images, 97, 132; Amr Nabil/AP Images, 98, 114; Nasser Nasser/AP
Images, 102; Khalil Hamra/AP Images, 104; Andrew Kaupang/iStockphoto, 106; Karen Moller/
iStockphoto, 111; Maya Alleruzzo/AP Images, 118; Tobias Helbig/iStockphoto, 123